THE
ENGLISH
CHALK STREAMS

THE
ENGLISH
CHALK STREAMS

SIDNEY VINES

B.T. BATSFORD LTD   LONDON

© Sidney Vines 1992
First published 1992

Typeset by Goodfellow and Egan, Cambridge
and printed and bound in Great Britain by
Butler and Tanner, Frome, Somerset
for the publishers
B.T. Batsford Ltd
4 Fitzhardinge Street
London W1H 0AH

A CIP catalogue record for this book is available from the British Library

ISBN 0 7134 6844 0

Frontispiece: The author fishing the Wylye

CONTENTS

ACKNOWLEDGMENTS

To the following, with whom it has been such fun to walk along their rivers, and talk about their fishing, I extend my grateful thanks.

Itchen Michael Baron, Robin Crawshaw (NRA), Ron Holloway, Mrs Impey, Peter Lapsley, Ron Wilton.

Test Bernard Aldrich, M. J. Burke, Anthony Edwards, John Fairey, Mark Firth, Vic Foot, Mrs Govett, John Halford, Alf Harper, Bill Hawkins, Cecil Hill, Jim Hunt, Leslie Kirby, Mick Lunn, Dave Morris, Mike Perry, David Rasch, Christopher Saunders Davies, David Steuart, Terry Smallbone, David Walford.

Meon Richard Stacey.

Avon Bill Bruce-Jones, Simon Cain, Steven Kemp, David Ransley, Val Swindale, Duncan Wilkinson (NRA), Gordon Topp.

Bourne (Wilts) Dr Darlow.

Bourne (Hants) Dave Morris.

Dever John Baker, Mark Ferguson.

Anton Charles Liddell, Michael Carke, Sean Wilson.

Nadder David Price, David Nickol.

Wylye Tony Hayter, David Nickol, Gordon Topp.

Frome Stafford Floyer-Ackland, John Fisher, Geoffrey Gallia, Mike Ladle, Christopher Rothwell.

Piddle Phillipa Sturdy, Richard Slocock.

Allen Harry Teasdale.

Kennet John Bankes (NRA), Dennis Boreham (NRA), John Goddard, Peter Ludlow, Steve Jones, Ted Hill, Don Macey, Michael Stratton, Neville Mutter, Peter Drake, Tony Taylor, Peter Woolnough, Frank Wilson, Bob Preston (NRA).

Pang Peter Trentham.

Lambourn Bob Preston (NRA).

Loddon Alan Gibberd.

Driffield Beck Robert Blair, Graham Mackrill, Stephen Madden, Denis Whitham.

Foston Beck Roger Bentley.

I would like also to extend particular thanks to the Countess of Malmesbury, without whose help my writing about the Test and Itchen would have been threadbare: to Dermot Wilson, who despite ill-health has given me the benefit of his unrivalled knowledge of the chalk streams: to Mrs Margot Jessop for her typing: and to my wife for her help and forbearance.

The publishers and author would also like to thank M. F. & G. Witherby for their permission to quote an extract from *A Ring of Wessex Waters* by John Ashley Cooper; Roy Eaton, Roy Shaw, Graham Swanson, Trevor Housby, and Dermot Wilson for their photographs (*RE* pp 72, 76, 79, 124, 139 and colour plates 5, 6, 7; *RS* pp 28, 156, 157, 159, 160, 163 and colour plates 8, 9; *GS* colour plate 4; *TH* colour plate 1; *DW*, pp 2, 12, 19, 23, 25, 35, 39, 48, 49, 53, 63, 69, 71, 81, 83, 92, 99, 101, 108, 113 and colour plates 2, 3; *Illustrated London News*, p 55); Carole Vincer for the maps; and Anthony Maynard for the line drawings.

LIST OF MAPS

PREFACE

This is a guide to the chalk streams, with the word 'guide' taken in the widest sense. It is a guide to the fishing and its development over the last century, and the state of the rivers today. But it seemed to me that to restrict the book to fishing alone would be too narrow: there is so much else of interest. It is of interest that at Wilton House, within a stone's throw of the Nadder, Shakespeare performed *Twelfth Night*: that we owe the Leckford fishery on the Test to John Spedan Lewis, founder of the John Lewis Group: that Winchester College is still educating boys in fly fishing and the classics, as it did Lord Grey of Fallodon, G. E. M. Skues, and Dermot Wilson. To paraphrase Dr Johnson: 'The man who is tired of the chalk streams is tired of life.'

Fishermen spend much of their time by the rivers baffled by the behaviour of the fish. They therefore turn avidly to the writings of such as Halford, Skues, and Sawyer, who offer some explanation of these mysteries. The men, and their writings, are discussed in these pages. The picture of Halford, in particular, which emerges is, I think, quite different from the popular image of a pompous, crusty, blinkered, old buffer – the ultimate dry fly purist. The real Halford was a more human and likeable man. Another sort of writer is the man who propounds no new theories, but simply communicates the joy of being by the chalk streams – such as J. W. Hills, Plunket Greene, and Howard Marshall. They, too, play a part.

As we who live by these rivers can see, and as the media tell us, the chalk streams are in decline. Some suffer from pollution from chemicals used in agriculture, or from fish farm effluent – though the situation here is improving. The major cause of decline is the abstraction of water from boreholes in the upper reaches of these

A skilled American visitor, George Mendoza, playing a trout
on the lower Test.

rivers which has resulted in parts drying up completely. The effects are worst in the smaller rivers like the Berkshire Pang or the Dorset Piddle. They are more vulnerable than the bigger rivers. At present, some ten per cent, at the most, of the chalk streams are unfishable for this reason: all is not yet lost. Another factor, of course, has been the exceptionally dry years of 1989 and 1990, especially the dry winters. The winter of 1991/92 has been dry again, and has exacerbated the problem.

The best hope for the future lies with the National Rivers Authority. This was set up in September 1989, when the Government found that without doing so, they could not privatise the water industry – which has not stopped them from claiming the credit for it! For the first time, we have a national body, adequately funded, whose sole *raison d'être* is the care of our rivers. It is showing signs of getting to grips with the problems, which are not insoluble. There is plenty of water in these islands, but not where we want it. Transporting it will be expensive and in the end we will have to pay. We must accept this, indeed demand it. The rivers belong to us all – not only fishermen and women.

Walking along the rivers, chatting to owners, managers, and keepers I have seen much that I do not like. I have seen fisheries that are over stocked and over fished. Stocking at the beginning of the season with a 'top up' after the mayfly, is one thing. Stocking every fortnight and including rainbows of a size that nature never intended is quite another. So is dividing the river into beats and fishing them seven days a week. Rivers should not be put under such pressure. It is a degradation of fishing.

And yet, despite everything, the chalk streams have never been more popular. A stretch of the Itchen (by no means the best part) was sold recently for £200 a yard (.9 m) double bank. In the seventies £20 a yard (.9 m) was considered a high price. This does not mean that the chalk streams are beyond the reach of the average angler. If one avoids the Test – where prices are absurd – there is plenty of good fishing available at a reasonable price. (See Price Guide on page 175.)

The setting of the chalk streams is still of surpassing beauty. There are still wild trout, if you look for them. There is still joy to be found on the chalk streams. Of course, I have a favourite river, and a favourite stretch on it, and it had occurred to me to name it, but then I recalled the story in Greek mythology of Paris, who was given a golden apple and asked to give it to the fairest of three goddesses. He did so, and started the Trojan War. On this matter, if on no other, my lips shall stay sealed.

I have only made the briefest mention of coarse fishing, although on some of the rivers, such as the lower Avon and the Kennet below Newbury, there is excellent coarse fishing. This is not because I regard coarse fishing as in any way inferior to fly fishing – far from it. It is more complex, for the coarse fisherman is dealing with several species. It requires a separate book. In the text, I have referred for convenience to 'fishermen'. This is not intended to exclude lady fly–fishers who, although outnumbered, can cause problems by their very excellence – as happened in Yorkshire (see pages 162).

Sidney Vines
Salisbury, August 1991

1

FISHING
THE CHALK STREAMS

Dermot Wilson, doyen of chalk stream fishermen and author of the modern
classic *Fishing the Dry Fly*, landing a brown trout at Easton,
one of the best stretches of the Itchen.

Chalk streams vary. Some like Tennyson's brook:

> wind about, and in and out
> with here a blossom trailing
> and here and there a lusty trout
> and here and there a grayling.

Some are fast flowing and some flow slowly. Some are deep (too deep to wade) and others flow, laughing and chuckling, over gravelly shallows. Some are far too wide to cast across, while others may be only 6 feet (1.82 m) wide (but can hold big trout). Some stretches, unlike Tennyson's brook, flow straight, almost like canals. The scenery too, varies from the open meadows of Hampshire to the chalk downs of Wiltshire, or heavily wooded stretches in all counties which by September are festooned with fishermen's lost flies.

These variations call for differing techniques, but the basic principles do not change. The object is to place an artificial fly or nymph in front of a fish so as to deceive him into believing that it is his natural food. It sounds simple, but it is not quite so simple as it sounds. After a lifetime of fishing, one is still learning. But there is no mystique about it, no magic. Even a novice (as long as he has learnt the basics of casting) will catch fish from time to time if he happens to be by the river when the fish are co-operative. Even the worst bridge player will take a trick if he has been dealt the ace of trumps.

But if you wish to progress beyond the novice stage, and really to enjoy the challenge of the chalk streams, remember this: fishing the chalk streams is a delicate art. The flies you use are tiny; they must land on the water delicately. The fisherman must move softly and quietly, whether on the bank or in the water. If the fish refuses your fly do not assume that it is because you are using the wrong one. It is far more likely that you are wrong. You have moved too noisily or too clumsily or too quickly, and he is aware of you. Once that happens, give up and move on. As G. S. Marryat put it: 'It's not the fly, it's the driver.' We shall discuss this matter of concealment later.

I do not think that casting can be taught satisfactorily in a book. The best way is to go to a qualified instructor, or study it on video, where you can watch an expert and replay it as often as you wish, and then practise in the garden. One point only is worth making: the essential requirement is to be accurate – that is, to land the fly within a foot or so of the fish at short distances of 10–15 yds (9.1–13.7 m). That is not too difficult, unless the wind is troublesome. Many beginners are obsessed with distance, particularly if they have learnt their fishing on still waters. Casting long distances on the chalk streams is seldom necessary, and it frightens intervening fish.

Finally, a word about catch and release, which is widely practised in the United States and is slowly increasing in popularity here in England. The more I think about it the more I like it, for it will reduce the practice of heavy stocking. One stretch of the Test, which used to receive 1000 trout a year 20 years ago, now receives 20,000. This has all sorts of adverse effects on the river and it de-grades the fishing. But to practise this properly, fishermen must use barbless hooks and learn how to release fish unharmed. We shall come to this too, later.

THE FISH

We are dealing here with three fish – the brown trout (*Salmo trutta*), the rainbow trout (*Salmo gairdneri*) and the grayling (*Thymallus vulgaris*). There are parts of some chalk streams which are good coarse fisheries, such as the Avon south of Salisbury, where the flow is sluggish and the bottom muddy, but they are beyond the scope of this book. Salmon run up some chalk streams to spawn and there are some important salmon fisheries in the lower reaches. They are dealt with in a separate section.

Brown Trout

It is not brown, as we all know, but as everyone knows it as 'the brown trout', it does not much matter. Sometimes its beauty, when newly caught and before *rigor mortis*, makes one gasp with amazement, tinged with regret at having killed a creature so magnificent. It has a silky iridescence, the steel grey back shading into golden, or sometimes silver flanks, the sides dappled with red spots.

It is the native fish of the chalk streams, and is the basic quarry. It is a loner. It takes up station in a favourite spot, where it can keep in position with the minimum of effort and see its food being carried down by the current, which it can then easily intercept.

Its food, fortunately for us, consists largely of flies or nymphs (to be discussed later) but trout are carnivorous and their diet is wide ranging, including each other. 'Don't ask me which trout are cannibals,' Frank Sawyer (1906–80, river keeper on the Avon for 52 years. See pp 91–94) used to say, 'they all are'. I have found the most extraordinary things in a trout's stomach: silver paper, cigarette ends (they seem to prefer cork tips), even on one occasion a mouse. But they will not eat anything rotten or decaying. The flesh can be white or pink, depending on their food. If the diet is mainly flies, the flesh will be white. If the diet is freshwater shrimps or crayfish, it will be pink. It will also be pink if the fish has been reared on pellets containing carotene in a fish farm and this is unfortunately the most likely reason for pinkness of flesh.

Rainbow Trout

The rainbow seldom breeds naturally in the chalk streams. From time to time they spawn successfully and rainbow fry are seen. Headlines appear in the angling press of the shock-horror type: 'Will rainbows take over the Test?' But within a year to two, they always die out. Long may this continue. It would be a disaster if rainbows took over and the brown became extinct.

Rainbows are, unfortunately, widely stocked in the chalk streams for mainly – though not entirely – commercial reasons. They grow faster than browns and are therefore cheaper. They are more spectacular fighters than browns in that they are more acrobatic – though the brown is equally courageous and determined.

They take the same flies and nymphs as do browns, and take up station much as browns do, but sometimes they shoal and have a tendency to wander, usually downstream. They are more brash and less cautious, take the lion's share of the food, and do not co-habit happily with the browns, which seem to sulk and lose condition.

I would rather they were not stocked into the chalk streams, but since they are, we must consider them. People say that they are easy to catch. This is only true when they are first stocked. They soon learn, by some primeval instinct, that man is a predator, and they have to be treated with respect. A careless cast will send them dashing for cover just like a wild brown.

Grayling

A lot of unkind things have been written about grayling – for instance, that while she is undoubtedly a game fish (it always seems right, for some reason, to call the grayling 'she' while the trout is always 'he') she is, like a Victorian governess, not quite a lady. Frank Sawyer, for much of his life, regarded them as vermin to be exterminated, but in his later years, after a trip to Austria, he wrote: 'In future I shall think more kindly of them on the Avon, where they must still be controlled, for I realise that these should be the fish of the cold, clear, waters of the mountains, and they are far from home'. In recent years, with the formation of the Grayling Society, the true worth of the grayling as a sporting fish has begun to be appreciated.

They spawn in April/May, and are in poor condition in midsummer, but by September they are in good fettle and give fine sport. The late well-known fisherman and writer, Oliver Kite (see pp 93–94), used to fish for them in October and fry them in butter by the riverside with wild mushrooms. He did this on television – it made your mouth water.

Grayling are more sensitive to pollution than trout and their disappearance is the first sign that something is wrong. They shoal, often in midstream and lie deeper than trout. They will come up to take a dry fly, but the more common method is to use a heavily weighted nymph such as the Killer Bug.

FLIES

The only reason for studying the natural fly is in order to deceive the fish into believing that your artificial is the natural fly on which he is feeding – in other words 'to match the hatch'. There is a school today which says that this is quite unnecessary: that presentation is all. If you can put your Black Gnat (or whatever) on the water properly, so that it sits up well cocked, and does not drag, and the fish can see it, it will take it – even if it is actually feeding on some other quite different fly.

This is partly true. Charles Ritz (who was a brilliant caster but no entomologist) used to say that the most important asset of a fly was that he (Charles Ritz) could see it. There is something in this, too. And nowadays the wide use of stocked fish means that they are less selective. Even wild fish, if they are hungry, can be tempted by a well-presented fly.

But there are many times when presentation is not all; times when even stocked fish are selective. The obvious example is the

Charles Ritz (1892–1976) was the son of César Ritz, who founded the Ritz Hotels in Paris and London. Immensely wealthy, he indulged a passion for fishing all his life. He was particularly interested in building rods and devised a split cane rod for nymph fishing as practised by Frank Sawyer.

midsummer evening rise, when the fish are definitely choosy. If they are taking sedges, even stocked fish will not take anything else. And by September, when they have become educated, all fish are choosy. The fisherman who is worth his salt will relish the challenge.

Those who decide to ignore entomology (defined as the study of insects) will still catch fish – but they will miss a fascinating part of the whole art of fly-fishing. So let us now consider the natural fly through the season.

The Natural Fly: The Three Families

If you are of a zoological turn of mind, and wish to study the entomology of the chalk streams, then you will be well rewarded. The fascination is infinite. But it is not necessary, to be a good exponent, to have more than a basic knowledge of the subject; and that can be acquired – like French – without tears. There are three basic families: Upwinged Flies (*ephemeroptera*), Sedges (*trichoptera*), and Flat Winged Flies (*diptera*).

Upwinged Flies

The life cycle is egg-nymph-dun-spinner. Trout eat them as nymphs, duns and spinners. The eggs hatch under water – from the river bed, from stones, or from weed stems. They hatch into nymphs, which behave in various ways, but for our purposes we are interested in those which swim about freely in mid water. This 'active nymph' stage can last days, weeks, or even months. Then the nymph decides that the time has come to hatch out into

a winged fly. How, with his minute brain does he assess the conditions of current, water and air temperature? He ascends to the surface, his outer body splits open and a winged insect, struggling and fluttering, emerges. If, in this vulnerable stage called a 'dun', they are not eaten by a fish or a swallow, then they fly off to rest on trees or plants near the river.

A few days later the sexes return, the males to engage in a mating dance over the water, the females to join them from time to time in order to mate. The process completed, the females dip over the water, dropping the fertilised eggs to begin the cycle again. They then fall exhausted and fluttering (hence the term 'spinners') to die and to be eaten by trout or birds. The males fly off into the woods to die, having fulfilled their duty, unwept, unhonoured, and unsung. It is not much fun to be a male ephemeroptera.

It is easy to tie artificials to imitate the active nymphs (two patterns suffice) and the hatching nymphs (at the most two patterns) and the female spinners (one pattern). The difficulty lies with the dun stage.

There are some 20 species on which the fish feed at different times of the day and season. Most books assume that they are easy to identify. I have found it at times impossible, especially if you are fishing from a high bank. If you are wading, then you can pick one off the water and examine it. If in doubt, you can narrow the possibilities by learning which flies are likely to be on the water at that particular time. People like Peter Lapsley, Dermot Wilson, and John Goddard, have listed their recommendations in their own books (see pages 168–169). I venture to give my own, below, based on 30 years of mixed success at the end of which I am still learning.

The Sedges

The sedges, with their folded-back wings, are easy to spot and to imitate. They are the flies most likely to appear on a summer evening, but in September they can also appear during the day. It is only the adult stage that we are interested in. The Grannom is an early season sedge, but of late years it has all but disappeared.

The Flat Winged Flies

Here the most important group is the midges. Their cycle is egg, larva, pupa, and adult. We are mainly concerned with the pupa, which hangs in the surface film, and which trout take avidly. Fishing the midge pupa has become more and more popular in recent years.

The black gnat is a useful name for several species, some of which breed on land, but fall on the water, and some good fishermen use them exclusively. I find them a useful stand-by. The hawthorn is a land based, early season fly, with long trailing legs. Oliver Kite relied on it to give him his limit on May Day.

—— RODS, TACKLE, AND CLOTHES ——

We are now equipped with flies, so let us consider what else we shall need. But first, let me give one word of advice from bitter experience: insure your tackle. Cars are broken into. Rods are forgotten in car parks and when the owner returns, it is too late. Insurance of fishing tackle is quite cheap.

Choose first not the rod but the line. The lighter the line, the more delicately it falls – but the more susceptible it is to wind. Frank Sawyer used AFTM 4. Dermot Wilson fishes lighter, and I admire his skill, but No. 4 is light enough for me, and I prefer weight forward to double taper for ease of casting. Buy the best quality line you can afford, it will repay you.

For general use the rod should be about 8½ ft (2.6 m), and

fairly stiff because for nymph fishing you need to strike fast. But not too stiff, because that will make delicacy difficult. If you are fishing one of the minor chalk streams, with a lot of trees and bankside vegetation, a short 7-ft (2.1 m) rod is an advantage. It enables you to fish below overhanging branches.

I cannot overemphasise the importance of a perfect marriage between the line and the rod. It is not enough to do this after a fashion, for then you will not realise the delight that a really good match can bring. It happened to me by luck a few years ago and all at once casting became a joy. Buy your line and reel, and

Brian Clarke first became well known as a stillwater angler but later, with his friend John Goddard, became interested in the chalk streams. Together they wrote *The Trout and the Fly* (1980).

arrange with the tackle shop to try out rods, one at a time, until you are satisfied.

Reels are of less importance. Their purpose is to hold the line and backing, and they should be big enough for that, not too heavy, and not too noisy in operation. Otherwise, reels are a matter of taste. Some are beautiful pieces of engineering: but this is not essential.

Braided leaders are a welcome innovation and I fully recommend them. The total length, including braid should be 9–11 ft (2.74–3.35 m) and the tip should be 2–3 lb (.9–1.3 kg) breaking strain. That is quite strong enough for normal purposes with the good quality nylon now on the market. Big fish of 4 lb (1.81 kg) can be landed without breakages: if these occur it is invariably caused by striking too fiercely. Stillwater fishermen may find this hard to believe, but I can assure them it is true. A 4-lb (1.81 kg) breaking strain is too thick, and too easy for the fish to see. But check with the rules of the fishery: if it is one stocked with 6 lb (2.72 kg) rainbows you will have to go thicker, and they may have a rule about minimum strength of casts.

A good landing net should have a circular metal frame (not a triangular one) and a telescopic handle. It should be carried in the middle of the back on a strong piece of heavy elastic cord – or a hook, if you are wearing a fishing vest. It should not be carried low at the side, where it will catch in nails on stiles, barbed wire, or prickly undergrowth and cause endless frustration. There are enough minor disasters in fishing without that.

A simple fly box made of colourless plastic divided into small compartments is all that is needed for dry flies. Never use one of those boxes with magnetised metal strips, which are alright for nymphs or wet flies. They squash the hackles of the dry flies, which are then useless.

A tin of silicon grease and some dry fly powder is required for drying flies. Put some powder in your palm and roll the fly gently in it. Then with finger and thumb, rub a little grease on the hackle fibres. Much better than floatants. A pair of small, sharp, blunt-nosed scissors for trimming nylon, a priest for dispatching fish quickly, a roll of spare nylon, completes the list of minor items.

There are various ways of carrying fish including, by string

through the gills, or in a bag. The bag should allow air to circulate, e.g. a straw bass bag. Never carry fish in a plastic bag – on a hot day, they will cook.

Polaroid glasses enable one to see into the water, as long as the sun is behind you, and this is an important factor in deciding which bank to fish from. At one time Oliver Kite thought that polaroid glasses gave fishermen an unfair advantage. Even great men can have aberrations, and he later accepted them as being fair.

The matter of clothing is quickly dealt with. Clothing must be drab in colour. The fisherman must blend into the background. I remember one man on a small lake, who was accompanied by his girlfriend in a brilliant white trouser suit. He did not catch any fish.

The old rubber thigh waders were hot to wear and clumsy to walk in. Now there are much better waders, with a short rubber boot and thin waterproof material up to thigh level. If your fishing involves a flight, take stocking-foot waders, which are light and small, in a suitcase, and wear a pair of canvas shoes.

FISHING THE DRY FLY

Early Season

The winter is over and gone. It is the time when 'the May month flaps its glad green leaves like wings, delicate filmed as new spun silk', in Thomas Hardy's words, and the fisherman has arrived, with joy in his heart, by the riverside.

Having put up your rod, and tied on an artificial fly appropriate to the season – let's say a Greenwell's Glory – you stand at the bottom of the beat and survey the scene. You hear the chiff chaff. Deep in the woods there is the drumming of a woodpecker. Golden buttercups abound. Having absorbed this, your eyes focus on the river, looking for signs of rising fish. Take your time. The river at first glance may seem dead, but look carefully. Look closely near the banks on both sides. Look behind and just in front of obstacles or weed beds. Rises may be tiny sips, hardly perceptible. Look on the edges of fast water. Food is carried down and the trout will wait for it, lying in the quieter water and moving out for a tasty morsel.

Move up the bank quietly. Do not be one of those who are in a hurry, always wanting to know what is round the next bend. They do not catch fish.

The Effect of the Weather

Trout do not, as a rule, rise when the air is colder than the water. They dislike putting their noses out into a colder element. Water temperature in the chalk streams is constant at 55°–60°F (12.7°–15.5°C) (except at extremes of heat in midsummer). It can often happen on a May morning that the air is colder – say around 40°F (4.5°C). By the middle of the day the air may have warmed up to 60°F (15.5°C). Then a rise is likely: until in the afternoon the air temperature falls and the fish go down. Rain makes no difference – it may even help, by making it more difficult for the fish to see you. I have known some splendid dry fly fishing in a day-long downpour. If the fishing is good you will forget all about the rain.

Why Didn't He Take?

You have found a rising fish. You see fly coming down and because it is early May you are expecting Large Dark Olives. They are indeed upwinged flies of an olive colour, so you decide to try your Greenwell's Glory size 12.

A fish can see a man standing upright behind him at 20 yds (18.2 m) – an astonishing fact. But below waist height you can approach much nearer. So crouching and finally kneeling, you get into position. The trout continues to rise. You lift the rod and begin to cast. Your fly falls short, but when you look you see the trout has vanished. Why? *He has seen the rod as it waved in the air.* This is a particular risk on a sunny day when there is a reflection from the varnish on the rod. There are two things that can be done. First, cast horizontally, or secondly – if it is possible – keep back from the edge so that the rod remains over land. Of course this makes an accurate cast more difficult. If these methods fail, then *keep further back downstream.*

Another possibility is that even if the fly fell short it fell too heavily with the line, disturbed the water, and frightened the fish. This is unlikely if the cast was too short, but it is certain if the cast was too long.

Suppose the fly passes over the fish and he refuses it? The

Dry-fly fishing for trout – note the kneeling position – on a Yorkshire beck.

obvious reason – that it is the wrong fly – is actually the least likely. First, it may not float properly. This is important, because the fly may look alright to the fisherman but not to the fish. The explanation is that the natural fly floats on its legs – usually six. The fish sees a circular group of indentations, or pimples in the water. This is the purpose of the hackle on a dry fly – to enable the artificial to float 'cocked'. After a minute or so on the water, the artificial will float waterlogged, with the body of the fly in the water and a steel hook below it. All but the most naive fish will be suspicious and if it continues to float over his head, he will pack up and move away.

Second, the artificial may drag. This is caused because the current flows faster or slower at different points across the stream. It ruins your chances of catching a fish. The dragging fly will rarely be taken, for the obvious reason that it is totally unnatural. But there are ways of avoiding it, by slightly altering the cast. Just before the fly lands on the water, check it. This will make it fall short, with a slack line which will take up some of the drag. Another method is to 'mend' line, i.e. to flick an upstream curve into the line as it lies on the water. These techniques can be mastered by anyone with a little patience. Most drag is plain to see – the fly skids on the water leaving a 'V'-shaped wake. But watch your fly carefully, if it is refused. It may be drag so slight that you can scarcely see it. But the fish can. His vision at a foot or so is very keen indeed – much keener than ours.

Thirdly, the fly may be the wrong size. There is no doubt that size matters greatly. Many times I have found that going down in size from 12 to 14, or from 14 to 16 or 18 produces results.

The only remaining possibility is that you are using the wrong fly. But in these particular circumstances of a morning in early May – it is so unlikely that we can almost rule it out.

To summarise, the fish did not take because:

a   He saw you
b   He saw your rod waving
c   Your line came down too heavily and scared him
d   Your fly was semi-waterlogged
e   Your fly dragged
f   Your fly was too big (or too small, but less likely)
g   It was the wrong fly.

The question arises – did the fish see the fly? A trout looks up through a 'window' in the surface of the water, outside which light is reflected downwards. The size of his window depends on his depth – the deeper he is, the bigger the window. As a general

guide I have found that if you place the fly within 18 in. (45.7 cm) of the fish, he is likely to see it.

By now, you may have decided that dry fly fishing on a chalk stream is far too difficult. Be reassured. In a round of golf, the worst performer will hit a really good shot when all comes right. It is the same thing with fishing – and this is what makes it all worthwhile.

The Mayfly

Every year, about the middle of May, the river-keepers' phones are busy. From boardrooms in the city of London they ask 'Has the Mayfly begun?' And if the answer is 'Yes', they cancel important meetings, make for their cars (where rods and tackle are already stowed) and set off for their favourite chalk stream.

Mayfly time generally lasts from about 14 May to 7 June: some chalk streams like the Kennet, are late. The Test has been getting earlier: in 1990, it began on 9 May.

A mayfly larva lies in the silt at the bottom of the river for two years (though exceptional conditions, such as a mild winter, can reduce this to one year), then hatches into a large nymph (about one inch long/2.5 cm) which rises to the surface and breaks open to become a dun, with wings, which flutters and struggles to escape the shuck and then flies off into nearby trees and bushes. There, it changes again into a spinner with beautiful white translucent wings. The male spinners dance in clouds, not over the water, but in nearby woods. The females join them, mating takes place, the females dip over the water laying eggs and then fall, spinning, on to the water to die. The males, their job done, also die, mostly on land. Apart from one brief happy moment, the male mayfly doesn't have much fun either.

The fisherman is interested in the dun and the spinner. Imitating the mayfly nymph is possible, but often banned. It is a large, weighty object and there is little finesse about fishing it. Orthodox doctrine is to wait until the nymphs hatch into duns. But if your time on the river is limited, it can be maddening not to be allowed to use it.

There should be little difficulty in putting on the water an artificial to represent the mayfly dun or spinner. But there can certainly be difficulty in persuading the fish to take the artificial, when there are hundreds of naturals on the water, and it is impossible to imitate the struggles of the dun to take off, or the spinning of the spent fly. 'Duffers' fortnight' is a gross misnomer. It can be easy of course – but not invariably.

The excitement of the mayfly is first, the miracle of nature that it is – the brief appearance of this beautiful fly in vast numbers, and second, the reaction of the fish once they realise what a dish is being set before them – Beluga caviare, and lots of it. They go berserk for it, taking with a savagery that is never seen at other times. Monsters who lurk in the depths and whose existence was never suspected, appear and feed with mad abandon. Of course it is thrilling. Who would want to be anywhere else in mayfly time but on a chalk stream?

Midsummer

The banks are lush with flowers, the willows and alders are in their glory. Bees buzz in the drowsy heat, and the fish seem to go to sleep too. This is the time of the evening rise, when the fun is crowded into one or two hours just before dusk. It can be frustrating. Fish rise everywhere but will not look at your artificial. There are two possibilities – the sedge or the spinner. Sometimes it starts with one and then changes to the other. Take a little torch for changing flies. This is a time when the fish *are* choosy, when your choice of fly does matter, and a little basic entomology makes all the difference.

On cooler days in June, after the mayfly, when fish might be expected to rise, they seldom do. It was said in the past by people who ought to have known better, that this was because the fish

were glutted with the mayfly. This is nonsense. A fish's digestion works in less than a day, after which his stomach is empty. The reason he does not rise is because there is nothing to rise to. The ephemeroptera – the olives and iron blues – hatch in May and again in August–September. But there are plenty of nymphs swimming in mid water, and caddis grubs on the bottom, and the fish are busily feeding on them. We shall consider nymph fishing later. But there is one fly that appears at this time, the Pale Watery, on cooler days in late June–July, and early August and it can provoke a rise. An artificial should always be carried (Tups).

Late Season

This is sometimes called the autumn reawakening. Daytime sedges appear, and you can use the delightful Lunn's Caperer. The excess heat is over, the flowers and birds are different (meadowsweet, willow herb). It is cooler, fish begin to rise in the daytime more often and the dry fly man is in his element again.

But there is one big difference from May. The fish are educated. The challenge is greater. They scare more easily. They will not take any old fly as they sometimes will in May. It must be the right fly, the right size and properly presented. But by this time the fisherman too should be in good practice with his skills honed by a season's fishing. It is a fair contest and in some ways the best of the whole season. Success in these conditions is all the sweeter.

A Final Word on the Dry Fly

After F. M. Halford published his great book *Dry Fly Fishing* in 1889 (see pages 73–75) there arose on the chalk streams a cult of the dry fly. These followers of Halford were so entranced by the new doctrine that they took it to absurd lengths. According to them the dry fly was the only ethical way to catch a trout. They became known as the dry-fly purists, or the dry-fly snobs.

There is nothing superior about dry-fly fishing. There is no such thing as 'the high art of the dry fly'. Its attraction lies in the fact that everything is there for the fisherman to see, even to the fish opening his mouth to take the fly. Why do we enjoy the dry fly so much? Simply because it is more fun than any other way of catching fish. That is all there is to it.

FISHING THE NYMPH

From the fisherman's point of view there are two distinct kinds of nymph fishing on the chalk streams – the hatching nymph in the surface film, and the sunk nymph which may be at any depth below the surface. They are the same insect at a slightly different stage (as will be explained) and the distinction may seem like splitting hairs. In a way it is, but on some fisheries you will find that the hatching nymph is allowed while the sunk nymph is not.

This rule applies on certain fisheries with large numbers of members, such as the Piscatorial Society, with stretches on the

Wylye, Avon, and Itchen. Such fisheries feel that if they allow the sunk nymph they open the door to the use of all sorts of ironmongery being dragged across the river, which would seriously damage the fishing. The word 'nymph' is loosely used today on stillwaters to describe things which are neither flies nor nymphs, but merely attracting lures.

On small syndicates, members usually agree among themselves, with the owners, on what they will use.

The Natural Nymph

It is possible to catch fish on a dry fly with the scantiest knowledge of entomology, but with the nymph it is essential to understand what you are doing – how the natural nymph fits into the scheme of things.

The upwinged flies evolve from egg to nymph to dun to spinner. The nymph stage can last days or weeks during which the nymph feeds on tiny plankton. Different species behave in different ways, but the ones we are interested in are known as free swimmers. They move about below the surface at all depths, swimming from weed bed to weed bed, or being carried along helplessly in the current, until the moment comes for them to hatch into a winged insect – the dun. They break the surface film, the shuck splits open and, fluttering, the winged insect emerges.

Fishing the nymph à la Skues

G. E. M. Skues was the first man to observe that fish apparently rising to dry flies were, in fact, taking hatching nymphs in the surface film. This was in 1910, thus nymph fishing on the chalk streams is a twentieth-century invention. A good imitation is the Gold Ribbed Hare's Ear nymph: the hackles along the body look like the wings emerging from the shuck. Peter Lapsley's idea of a Pheasant Tail nymph tied with silk instead of wire is also effective for the nymph a few moments earlier in its existence, before the shuck opens. Skues himself devised a multiplicity of patterns –

Leigh Perkins, President of the Orvis Co. Inc., fishing the smooth waters at Kimbridge on the Test.

18 in all – for his Abbotts Barton fishery on the Itchen. This is quite unnecessary. Nobody bothers with such exact imitation nowadays.

The method with the 'damp' or hatching nymph is exactly the same as the dry fly. The nymph is cast 2–3 ft (.6–.9 m) in front of the trout and allowed to drift down over him. The same considerations of drag etc. apply. This method is only really effective on smooth water, such as Skues' water at Abbotts Barton on the Itchen, when the take can be clearly seen.

The Midge Pupa

The midge pupa is not, strictly speaking, a nymph at all, though it is fished like a Skues' hatching nymph. It is the pupa of many species of flat winged flies. All we need to know is that the natural pupa hangs just below the surface film, prior to its hatching into a winged insect. It is one of the trout's basic foods – its bread and butter. Most of the authorities recommend it for a summer evening, but I have found it effective in almost all conditions. Obviously your chances are best if the fish can be seen. If it cannot, grease the cast to within 3 in. (7.6 cm) of the pupa and watch for a slight check.

Fishing the nymph à la Sawyer

When we come to the sunk nymph, we find a different style altogether. It is known, after the late Frank Sawyer, as the Netheravon style. Imitating the natural nymph is easy. Only two patterns are needed – the ubiquitous Pheasant Tail for the olives and the Grey Goose for the pale wateries. Both were devised by Frank Sawyer. Both are tied with fine copper wire to make them sink, and have no hackles. Imitation is easy, but problems remain. First where and how to cast the nymph, second how to imitate the natural's behaviour, and third how to strike.

The nymph must be cast further upstream than a dry fly because it must be allowed to sink to the fish's level. This obviously depends on the current, and on the fish's height in the water, and requires fine judgement. A fish will often look upwards, but seldom down. The cast itself is different. Unlike the delicate landing which we try for with dry fly, the nymph must be 'pitched' to hit the water and sink. Those whose dry flies habitually land with a splash will find it easy!

Natural nymphs can swim. They dart about on the edges of weed beds. But they are also sometimes carried down by the current. So decide how far you want your nymph to sink, and grease the cast accordingly. Let the artificial swim down with the current. If you can see the fish (which is the most exciting situation) watch his mouth. If it opens and you see white, strike instantly. Fish can see further in the water than they can on the surface, and will sometimes swim 3–4 ft (.9–1.2 m) to take a nymph. Then you can see it all – the mouth open, the jaws close on the nymph, the strike. Thrilling!

Immediately before taking the nymph the fish will often rise slightly in the water. If you see this, strike. In nymph fishing fish are more often lost through striking too late than too early; for as soon as the fish tastes the artificial, he spits it out – and he does this very fast indeed. If you cannot see the fish, watch the end of the cast where it enters the water. Concentrate one hundred per cent on it, and if you see the slightest check – strike. This method is not infallible, for there are times when a take happens but gives no indication on the cast. Nothing can be done about this, but if you believe a fish is there, it is worth trying the induced take, as propounded by Oliver Kite. As the nymph approaches the fish, raise the rod tip slightly, enough to lift the nymph in the water and give the illusion of life. It is a satisfying way to catch a fish and is effective around the edge of weed beds.

In nymph fishing, you need to strike fast – much faster than with a dry fly – but not fiercely. If you are using a fine point (as you should be) you risk a break. A better word than strike is 'tighten'. If, like me, you find it hard to resist the instinctive strike, I like Peter Lapsley's advice to let go of the line with the left hand (if you are fishing right handed). That way you are less likely to break.

The main difficulty in nymph fishing is in timing the strike. With a dry fly, you can see the take: with a nymph it is less obvious. But you will find after a time, you will develop a sixth sense which tells you when to strike. I catch more fish on a Pheasant Tail nymph than in any other way – though the midge pupa is beginning to rival it.

———— FISHING FOR GRAYLING ————

As I have already mentioned (see page 18) the time to fish for grayling is September up to Christmas, especially in those lovely autumn days of October, when the leaves are golden and the skies are a bright cold blue.

The basic methods are the same as for trout, but they tend to lie deeper, nearly on the bottom, and a really weighty nymph is needed to get down to them. Letting a Killer Bug out through a shoal, and then using the Induced Take, can be deadly. Oliver Kite, using this method, used to catch them blindfolded and with a bare hook.

———— CATCH AND RELEASE ————

There has been much discussion about the merits of a policy of catch and release, but little about the proper way to do it. A fish carelessly handled, played to exhaustion, with the hook torn out, will most likely die. If it survives, it will become uncatchable.

There is a right way, and it is as follows. First, always use barbless hooks. It is a simple matter to flatten the barb with a pair of blunt-nosed scissors or pliers. Be firm with a hooked fish, bring it in as soon as you can. Reel in until the fish is in the water an inch or two (2.5–5 cm) from the tip of the rod. Shake the rod, and in 90 per cent of cases the fish will come off. If it doesn't, the next best alternative is to run your hand down the cast until you can hold the hook shank. Give it a twist and the fish will be free. If you cannot do this, say because the bank is too high, then the net must be used, the fish lifted out, the hook removed (hold the fish upside down and it will not struggle) and the fish gently returned to the water. If you can, make sure that he is upright.

Done properly, he will swim away and will soon have forgotten an unpleasant, but short and comparatively painless, episode.

Landing a fish on the middle Test, which is big for a chalk stream. Note the
fish is brought over the net, not the net under the fish.

SALMON

The late John Ashley Cooper was the leading authority on
salmon fishing in the chalk streams. The following extract from
his book *A Ring of Wessex Waters* is reprinted with the permission
of his publishers, H. F. & G. Witherby Ltd.

The fish are inclined to prefer deep holes or deep pools. They
do not like the shallows, but are usually found in water of four

feet [1.2 m] or more in depth, either at the neck or tail of the deeps. It is difficult for someone who does not know the river to judge where the lies are likely to be . A pronounced bend is apt to produce a lie, and where the current is steady flowing rather than boiling. On the other hand, boils on the surface indicate weed clumps or outcrops of some sort on the bottom and fish sometimes like to lie upstream of these, or to one side of them. And where there are hatches, fish usually pause, either above them, or downstream in the tail of the main rush, or in the backflow on either side under the bank.

It must be admitted that fish seldom show on the Avon, and one never finds a pool of jumping fish, as for instance on some well stocked Highland river. In actual fact, it is rare to see an Avon★ fish show at all: and if one is seen, it is worth fishing over where it showed, even if this looks an unlikely place. The fish *may* be a runner, but it may not – and if not it will probably take. To sum up on this question of finding lies, the whole process to a newcomer is a difficult one, and experience is by far the best teacher.

Spring fish still run large, averaging around 16–17 lb [7.2–7.7 kg]. Nylon monofilament of a minimum breaking strain of 15 lb [6.8 kg] is needed, and 20 lb [9.0 kg] is often better. In summer, it is unwise to use less than 10 lb [4.5 kg] breaking strain, and 12 lb [5.4 kg] is none too light. There is

★ Written of the Avon, but equally applicable to Itchen, Test, or Frome.

nothing more infuriating than to be broken by a good fish through the use of too fine a cast or trace.

Now some words on the process of fishing. Undoubtedly, Avon salmon are more easily caught on bait rather than on fly. The causes of this are many. Usually the stream is too slow for a fly to fish attractively, also the fish are apt to lie too deep for them to rise readily to a fly near the surface.

A bait, on the other hand, can be fished slowly and almost down to their mouths. Another disadvantage of fly is that fish often lie close under an almost perpendicular bank. Thus the fly, from whichever side it is fished, cannot swing over them (which is such an effective tactic in the open pools of a north country river). A bait on the other hand, at least if it is fished from the deep side, can be brought attractively to within inches of the fish's mouth and, if necessary, held there.

Floating weed during weed cutting periods is also a hazard to fly fishing, as it is to bait fishing but more so. It is easier for the bait fisherman to manoeuvre his line to dodge such pieces of weed. A fly fisherman fishing near the surface can find this almost impossible.

All these factors combined make it difficult to catch a fish on a fly, and a bait fisherman almost always has a better chance of success. The result is that bait fishermen on this river by far outnumber fly fishermen, and it is safe to say that eleven out of twelve Avon salmon are caught on bait of one sort or another. Baits most frequently used are wooden Devon minnows and Toby or Mepps spoons, while prawns, shrimps, plugs and worms, (if allowed) are used extensively.

Fishing in the Avon is all from the bank: there is virtually no wading, except on occasions at knee depth on a sandbank. Gumboots, or at most thigh waders are all that is needed. A gaff is the only effective instrument for handling a big fish when the angler is by himself. A landing net is alright for

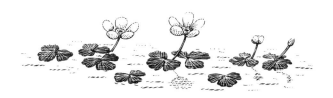

grilse, but not for anything over 20 lb [9.0 kg]. A priest is also something that every angler should carry, and a pair of polaroid glasses. The actual process of fishing is much the same on the Avon as on other salmon rivers, with one important exception. It pays on this river, as on the Frome and Test, to fish very slowly, ie not to hurry in paying out the cast, and often to let the bait hang for some moments in a likely lie. Even more important is take only a short step downstream between successive casts. One has often heard the theory that 'it is better to fish a pool down twice quickly than once slowly'. That may well be true on north country rivers, but it is certainly not true on south country rivers such as the Avon, Frome, and Test. On these, one can hardly fish too deliberately, and one needs to proceed very carefully and very slowly, yard by yard, and almost foot by foot. In addition, one needs great accuracy in casting when fish are lying close to the opposite bank. The fly or bait has to drop not within feet but within *inches* of the far side if it is to stand any chance. This is a factor of the greatest importance.

If you rise or pull a fish, give him a minute or so before you try again. The point of this is to give him time to return to his lie. Never be in too much of a hurry. Playing hooked fish is comparatively simple. They seldom have room to run out a long line, and with the heavy tackle used in spring it is a rather brutal business.

As already mentioned, it is difficult to catch salmon on a fly in the Avon, but by no means impossible. In early spring, if the angler wishes to use fly, he needs heavy tackle. A carbon rod of 16 ft [4.88 m] is neither too long nor too heavy, and a slow sinking line or a floater with a sink tip is wanted. A big tube fly on a brass body with hair wing is the best lure, on nylon of a least 15 lb [6.8 kg] strength. A rod of such length is desirable, partly because the wind can be troublesome, and partly because it gives better control of line and fly as they are fished round. Later in the season, a rod of 14 ft [4.26 m] or even 13 ft [3.96 m] will be found adequate, though there is no harm in using a longer rod if this is preferred. Flies can be smaller, on double or treble hooks, but size 6 is the smallest one ever needs. A good fly reel is desirable, with 100 yds [91.4 m] of 20 lb [9.0 kg] backing.

When fishing a floating line, the angler should watch for a V or boil in the water, indicating that a fish has moved at his fly without touching it. Mark the place, and return to the fish later.

Finally a word as to water temperature. Cold water of, say, 43°F [6.1°C] or less means large flies and baits: but as it gets warmer the size should lessen, until when it reaches 60°F [15.5°C] all lures should be fairly small. For fly fishing, a floating line becomes desirable when the temperature reaches 52°F [11.1°C]. To a large extent, therefore, the water temperature provides a ready-reckoner for the choice of fly or bait: but when the air is markedly colder than the water the fish take badly and need a lure well sunk.

THE ITCHEN AND MEON

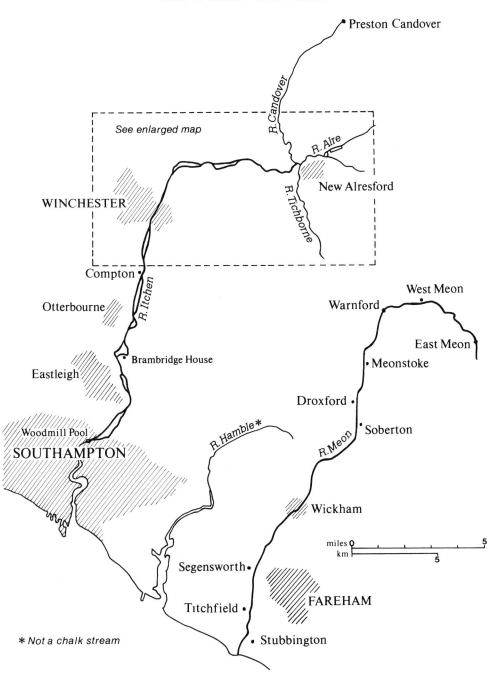

Preston Candover

R. Candover

R. Alre

WINCHESTER

See enlarged map

New Alresford

R. Tichborne

Compton

West Meon

Warnford

East Meon

Otterbourne

R. Itchen

Meonstoke

Brambridge House

Droxford

Eastleigh

Soberton

Woodmill Pool

R. Hamble *

R. Meon

SOUTHAMPTON

Wickham

miles 0 _____ 5
km _____ 5

Segensworth

FAREHAM

Titchfield

* Not a chalk stream

Stubbington

2

THE RIVERS OF HAMPSHIRE

Itchen

Test
(including Bourne, Dever, Anton and Dun)

Meon

THE ITCHEN

After two years of blazing hot summers and dry winters, the Itchen has so far suffered surprisingly little. It remains what it has always been – an enchanting river.

There are a number of reasons for this, such as the absence of a major town near the source, and meadows along the banks rather than ploughed fields, but the Itchen compensation scheme has undoubtedly been the major factor. Bore holes were sunk into the chalk downs near Preston Candover and near the Alre a few years ago, and water is pumped up into the river whenever the flow falls below a certain level. The purpose of the scheme was not to benefit the fishing – that was incidental – but to ensure the quality of the drinking water taken near the mouth by the Portsmouth Water Co. Two miles above, near Eastleigh, is a large sewage works, and it is essential that there is enough flow to dilute the sewage outfall.

The scheme depends on winter rains refilling the aquifers below the downs at Preston Candover. As long as that happens, this imaginative piece of water engineering can continue indefinitely.

From the Source to Winchester

The three streams which form the Itchen are the Tichborne, the Alre, and the Candover Brook. They come together just west of New Alresford to form the Itchen. They have been well described as 'small but perfect editions of minor chalk streams'. Fish farms have made their unwelcome appearance on the Tichborne and the Alre, but still for most of their length the water is crystal clear and they provide fine dry fly fishing.

And so we come to the Itchen proper – the six miles (8 km) which flow west from New Alresford to Winchester – and are generally considered to be the best, not only for the fishing, which is superb, but for the enchantment of the setting. Everything is gentle - the slope of the downs, the meadows and the spinneys, the flow of the river as it winds in and out. Here are

THE UPPER ITCHEN

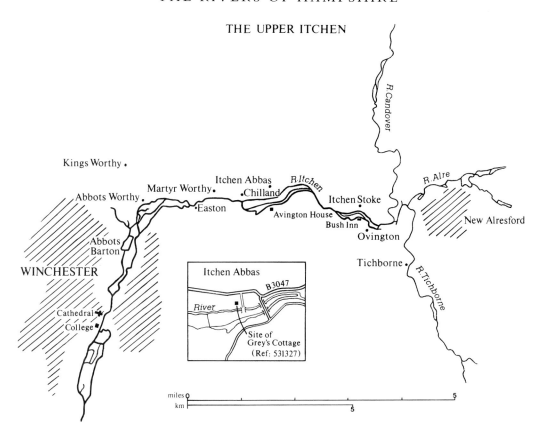

meadowsweet, and rose bay willow herb, and the yellow irises of May. The twentieth century may have brought change, decay and ugliness – but this valley remains untouched and unsullied.

Two miles (3.2 km) west from New Alresford along the B3047 is the village of Itchen Abbas. There used to be a railway station here, and Sir Edward Grey, who was Foreign Secretary from 1905 to 1916, would catch the train at Waterloo at 6 am on a Saturday, alight at Itchen Abbas, walk half a mile (.8 km) to his cottage on the river bank, pick up his rod, and go fishing. There is a lot to be said for the train.

Grey describes all this in his classic *Fly Fishing*, first published in 1899. The cottage was burnt down in 1923, but the foundations and a chimney stack remain, and today one can still see the river as he, looking out of his bedroom window, must have seen it.

Grey produced some fine, elegant writing in *Fly Fishing* and it

A particularly beautiful part of the Itchen.

is apparent that he loved the Itchen: but he was not a good enough observer to be a great fishing writer. For this you need a dispassionate, logical, analytical mind, plus a dogged determination to unravel nature's mysteries. Halford, Skues, and Sawyer were men with these qualities, as we shall see, but Grey was not. For all his abilities he was a dilettante.

Across the river from Grey's cottage lies Avington House, a stately home which once belonged to the Duke of Buckingham, but is now divided into flats. Here Charles II and Nell Gwyn dallied, because the Bishop of Winchester indicated that Nell was *persona non grata* under his roof. Charles II was a keen sportsman, *vide* the Rowley Mile at Newmarket, but I doubt that he found the time to go a-fishing. There is no record that he did.

Westward one mile (1.6 km) from Itchen Abbas is the hamlet of Chilland. Here just north of the river is an old mill which was once a trout hatchery of historic significance. From here, in the 1870s, trout ova were exported (carefully packed in ice) to Australia, Tasmania, and Kashmir, to start brown trout populations there.

West from Chilland is the well-known Martyr Worthy fishery owned by Mr Simon Ffennell and keepered by Mr Ron Holloway, whose proud claim it is that the river has not been stocked since 1926. A great deal has been done to encourage natural spawning by raking the gravel redds and directing the current by careful weed cutting. Apart from this, the main reason that stocking has been avoided is the policy of Mr Ffennell, only to fish the river lightly. There are few rods, and it is one of the most expensive of the chalk stream fisheries. Thus, with light pressure on the river, the fishing has been kept natural. Keeping it at a high standard can also be hard work. Over the years, all chalk streams tend to erode their banks. The river has to be narrowed. It is back-breaking work at the best of times, when the earth or chalk can be brought to the bank by machine. Picture Mr Ffennell and

The upper Itchen at Easton, a medium-sized stream at this point. Note the angler has a straw bass bag for carrying fish. It is loosely woven and allows air to circulate.

Mr Holloway moving ten tons of earth, a wheelbarrow load at a time. That is devotion.

Next, at Easton, is a fishery owned by a private syndicate and immortalised in Janet Marsh's charming *Nature Diary* which describes all variety of the flora and fauna to be seen there, through the changing seasons. Below this, Orvis have a stretch of almost a mile, which is available for letting. It is heavily fished, and therefore heavily stocked. But the setting is all that one could desire.

After the Orvis water, is the 1½ miles (2.4 km) (including carriers) belonging to the Piscatorial Society, founded in 1836 in London by a group of friends who decided to form an association 'to promote and encourage fair angling and to stimulate harmonious social conversation'. Over more than 150 years they have flourished. They like to call themselves guardians of the chalk streams: they never stock rainbows; they always try to encourage the growth of wild or at least thoroughly naturalised brown trout – and generally succeed. We shall find them again, on the Avon and the Wylye.

This is the last of the upper Itchen valley fisheries, for we are now close to the city of Winchester. Apart from the Orvis water, it is all non-commercial, fished by syndicates or clubs who let season rods only. If there were any other system, it would not be so good.

Winchester and the Middle Itchen

The Itchen where it runs through Winchester is very pleasant, and there is a public footpath along the bank. It helps the cultural life to have a magnificent cathedral, and that of Winchester, whose construction was ordered by William the Conqueror in 1079 (the third building on the site) is one of the glories of European civilisation. Izaak Walton is buried in a chapel in the south transept. He died in Winchester in 1683, aged 90, in the house of his son-in-law Dr William Hawkins, who was a prebendary of the cathedral. Walton did not fish the Itchen, for he was too old when he came to live in Winchester, but no river fits more perfectly the spirit of serene contemplation with which *The*

IZAAK WALTON
1593 - 1683

'Study to be quiet...'

Compleat Angler is imbued. On a wall in the nave is a plaque to
Francis Francis (1822-1886) a great angler of the Victorian age.

Apart from the cathedral, the other major institution of the city
is Winchester College. But before we arrive, there is a fishery of
historic significance on the northern outskirts – Abbotts Barton.

Abbotts Barton

Just where, to the north-east of the city, the Itchen turns south,
lies the Abbotts Barton fishery, where G. E. M. Skues fished for
56 years up to 1938, and where he developed the theories of
nymph fishing which he expounded in two classic books (*Minor
Tactics of the Chalk Stream*, 1910 and *The Way of a Trout with a Fly*,
1921) and which have made his name immortal. Here, in the
1890s, came F. M. Halford (Skues did not think much of his
technique: he says Halford's gut was too coarse), Francis Francis,
R. S. Hall (inventor of the eyed hook), William Senior (Editor of
The Field), and that strange figure G. S. Marryat who wrote
nothing but was highly esteemed by the others. Halford, some

say, borrowed his ideas. Fishing at Abbotts Barton is like going out to bat at Lords in the footsteps of W. G. Grace, Jack Hobbs, and Len Hutton.

The fishery consists of about a mile (1.6 km) of the main river, with two side streams running parallel, originally part of the old water-meadow irrigation system – about 3 miles (4.8 km) fishing in all. The stretches are almost straight, like canals, with no shallows where the water ripples over gravel. The river runs straight and smooth through open, flat meadows. The whole fishery is sandwiched between a dual carriageway (the A33) and the busy main road north from Winchester. The gasworks of Skues' day have been replaced by an industrial estate, and the centre of the city is less than a mile away.

Still, none of it is intrusive – the ugliness is screened by trees. The water meadows are flat, but pleasant enough. It provides the peaceful refuge which all fishermen require: but the setting does not compare with the ineffable beauty, the sheer loveliness, of the Itchen only a mile or two upstream. Why, then, did Skues fish here for 56 years? I think, for two reasons. First, the quality of the fishing is superb, with prolific fly life. And, because the surface is usually smooth, it is ideal for fishing the nymph in, or just below, the surface film. You cannot do it in rough water. Secondly, Skues, it seems to me, was not very interested in flora and fauna. If a kingfisher flew past, I doubt if he would have seen it. His eyes would have been on the river. Skues spent his life, when he was not working as a solicitor, catching fish. Not for the pleasure of killing – most of them he returned to the water. It was the intellectual and aesthetic challenge which fascinated him. He was the first to see that a trout which appears to be rising may really be feeding under the water, taking nymphs in or below the surface film. The discovery could only have been made by a man with acute powers of observation, good knowledge of entomology, and an analytical mind. All this, Skues had and he is deservedly immortal.

At the end, Skues was a lonely and embittered man. He quarrelled with the other members of the Abbotts Barton syndicate because they wanted to stock, and he didn't, and they said he could only invite guests if they shared his rod. In the discussion, he says he was in a minority of one.

One can read between the lines. Skues did not want to stock because, being a far better angler than the others, he would catch fish while they could not. This would have irritated them. Skues constant habit of bringing down guests would have irritated them further. And after more than half a century, he would have

The Itchen at Abbots Worthy. Dermot Wilson lands a fish.
This is now Piscatorial Society water.

expected to get his own way. When he did not, and was outvoted, he resigned in disgust. It was very sad. Skues must have been exasperating, but the members might have put up with him for the few years that were left.

In the 1960s, the fishery fell into decline. It was rescued in 1974 by Mr Roy Darlington, who says that, like Skues, he fell under its spell. With his brother, he set to work, and now the river is in first class condition. Hatches of fly are quite exceptional. Fish rise most of the day in most conditions. Even when they do not – in summer heat – there is an explosive evening rise to make up for it.

The Winchester College Water

In 1907, Dr Burge, then Headmaster, decided that the College ought to own the fishing rights on the Itchen where it passed through the College grounds. Sir Edward Grey was approached and provided the finance. Since then, Winchester has owned its own fly fishing and, by implication, has regarded it as a part of a boy's education. We all know about the battle of Waterloo being won on the playing fields of Eton. If the battle for twentieth-century industrial supremacy was lost on the banks of the Itchen, then so be it.

The college was founded in 1382 (long before Eton, as they are keen to tell you) by William of Wykeham - hence the term Wykehamist.

When Skues and Grey, both young Wykehamists, fished the water in the 1870s, they bought day tickets from Mr Hammond, who kept a tackle shop in the square. Hammond was succeeded by Mr Chalkley who is remembered with affection by generations of boys. Grey's account of his fishing at Winchester is, in my opinion, the best part of his rather disappointing book. The first year, the trout defeated him, but he observed the great men fishing. There was Francis Francis, with his 14-ft (4.2 m), greenheart rod who, according to Skues, cursed a lot, William Senior, Editor of *The Field* and G. S. Marryat who Grey describes as 'the greatest angler I have ever met'. In his first year, he caught only one trout: they were to wily for him. But in his fourth year, having been helped by Marryat, he caught 76.

Viscount Grey of Fallodon (1862–1933), who when Foreign Secretary
(1905–1916) used to travel by train early on Saturday mornings from
London to Itchen Abbas, walk half a mile (.8 km) to his cottage,
and be on the river before 9 a.m.

Boys fish the waters today much as Skues and Grey did and as
Dermot Wilson, in his time, also did. There is a footpath from
Garnier Road along the river into the city. The playing fields and
college buildings are on one's left and a nature reserve beyond the
river to the right. Ahead is the cathedral. It is a pleasant stroll,
truly *rus in urbe*. A don, Mr Michael Baron, has cared for the river
for the last 30 years, and there is a bailiff. It is in fine condition.

The Lower Itchen

Below Winchester, the surroundings change. There are more buildings. There are more people. Instead of charming villages, a once attractive place like Otterbourne has become an overblown suburb of Southampton. The otters have gone, and so has the charm. It lacks the glamour of the great names, which add lustre to the upper Itchen. The fishing is more commercially exploited. On one stretch, there are 'corporate hospitality' days, when large companies entertain their clients to a day on a chalk stream. The fastidious Grey would have been horrified. There is more stocking of fish of a takeable size and there is good dry fly fishing down to Eastleigh. But it is not, like the upper Itchen, superb.

There are about a dozen fisheries between Winchester and Eastleigh, all either in private hands or clubs such as the Bishopstoke Fly Angling Club. There is one house of historic importance – Brambridge House, a stately home near Otterbourne with picturesque gardens sloping down to the Itchen. Mrs Maria Fitzherbert lived here. She was the mistress of George IV, and later his morganatic wife. The King, who was first Prince Regent when his father George III was declared mad, and who built the Royal Pavilion at Brighton, used to visit Mrs Fitzherbert at Brambridge. George IV was a keen angler, mostly for pike in the lake at Virginia Water. The rods and tackle made for him by Ustonson of London can still be seen at Kew Palace. The present house on the site, now converted into flats, dates from 1873.

The last 3 miles (4.8 km) of the Itchen, down to the sea at Southampton, is a salmon fishery, divided among several owners. The most productive is Woodmill Pool, situated in a park within the city of Southampton, which is fished both by net and rod. In 1989, the total catch was 430 salmon, of which the rods caught 359. This was a below average year.

One major change has occurred since the days of Grey and Skues, not so much in the river as in the people who fish it. No longer are they solely leisured gentlemen from the 'upper crust', or even professional people like Skues. It is almost classless now, with many local business people owning water or taking rods for a season. If anything, they care for the river better than did their forebears. The Itchen will always inspire devotion.

THE TEST

The Test is far and away the biggest of the chalkstreams – not so much in width, although there are places too wide to cast across, but in every other way. Although it is only about 30 miles (48.3 km) direct by road from the source at Overton to the mouth at Southampton, it provides, with tributaries, at least 120 miles (193 km) of fishing. This is because, over the centuries, man-made channels for irrigation purposes have resulted in two, or sometimes even three, parallel streams, all fishable.

The literary heritage is also richest on the Test. The names of Richard Durnford, Peter Hawker, Plunket Greene, John Waller Hills, and F. M. Halford come to mind. Their writings have given the Test a special stature in the world of fly-fishing which it can never lose – even if its present state is a decline from past glories. So let us journey down the river, considering the different stretches and the towns and villages, and the famous men associated with them, as we go.

The source to Whitchurch

In 1712, the Huguenot family of Portal began to make paper at Bere Mill on the Test (where the keeper Mr David Walford, now lives). This developed into the large industrial complex at Overton where they make banknotes for the world. The firm is called Portal Holdings and is headed by Mr Julian Sheffield. The Portal fishery runs for 4½ miles (7.2 km) from the source to just before Whitchurch. The fishing is private, for tenants of the estate and company guests. There have been exceptions: Oliver Kite had a rod there, which he greatly prized, and died there on the bank near Overton of a heart attack on 15 June 1968. It was the way, and the place, that he would have chosen.

Mr Walford has a small trout farm at Bere Mill which supplies fish to other fisheries. He stocks his own river with fry, which grow up into wild fish. The Test here is a young stream, a mere stripling compared to the blowsy dowager we find lower down. Water abstraction and long droughts give cause for concern. In

THE TEST

and the Hampshire Bourne, Anton, Dever, Wallop Brook & Dun.

the winter of 1990–91, the top mile at Overton was dry.

Still, there is enough water between Overton and Whitchurch to provide fine fishing, as delicate an art as a purist could wish – wild, wary, trout, and tiny flies on 7X casts. There is no mayfly here, no grannom, and no iron blue, but this is made up by plentiful olives, blue-winged olives, pale wateries, and sedges. And no rainbows!

Whitchurch (pop. 4,000) is a quiet little Hampshire town with a long history. There is a silk mill still operating, using power from a water wheel, and fine healthy trout can be seen in the millstream, accepting titbits from visitors. The White Hart, a hostelry since 1461, was used by Charles Kingsley and Plunket Greene as a base for fishing – and it still is a good base.

From Whitchurch To Stockbridge

The first fishery is that owned by Mr 'Chips' Keswick (1¾ miles/ 2.7 km). Mr Keswick does not let rods. He stocks lightly – unfortunately, including rainbows – but most of the fishing is for wild fish. Below this is the Tufton fishery of 2¼ miles (3.6 km) including a carrier, fished by a syndicate of seven rods who fish named days and are allowed two guests per day. The carrier is a perfect miniature chalk stream of clear, sparkling water running over gravel, while the main river has everything one could wish – slow running, fast stretches, shallows, deeps, and hatch pools which must be very heaven on a June evening. There is good natural spawning supplemented by 700 stocked browns. The keeper, Mr Leslie Kirby, is an ex-Water Authority bailiff who knows his job, and more important, loves his river. The Tufton fishery is exceptional.

The Bourne Tributary

Now we digress from the main Test to the little Bourne, which enters the Test just below Tufton, immortalised by Harry Plunket Greene in *Where the Bright Waters Meet*. He wrote of it: 'Only three miles in all, but those three miles a dry-fly fisherman's paradise!' Of the valley and the village of Hurstbourne

Priors he writes: 'It ran through one of the fairest valleys and prettiest villages in the south of England … it ran twisting and turning, fast and smooth, under trees and in the open, chaffing and laughing itself into your very heart.'

Harry Plunket Greene was an Irishman, born in Dublin in 1865, and there is a Celtic lilt to his writing. At its best, it has a magical charm which no one else has matched. He poured his heart out with joy at the little river, the trout, the golden buttercups, and the friends Wyld, Savage, and Sharkey who shared it. What fun they had, in those Edwardian days of 1905, when the world was secure, and peace and progress would go on for ever.

I have often wondered how good a fisherman he was. As a sportsman he had a good eye, and good reflexes, but his knowledge of entomology seems to have been scant. There was only one fly for him – the Iron Blue – and he adored it to the exclusion of all else. This, of course, does not matter. Flyfishing is all about having fun – otherwise, why do it? And no one could communicate the joy of it all better than Plunket Greene.

What of the Bourne today? Not completely ruined, but a mixture. The bottom, where the bright waters actually meet, is unchanged, and still lovely. Upstream half a mile (.8 km) to the Beehive Bridge, it is good. This stretch is owned by the newspaper magnate Mr Jocelyn Stevens (also Chairman of English Heritage), and is well maintained. Rods are let by the Rod Box of Winchester. The village of Hurstbourne Priors has been spoiled by infilling of suburban villas, and the Cascades behind the church, once a beauty spot, are a sad sight of neglect, with fallen trees everywhere. Further up, the Iron Bridge is the same picture of neglect. The sawmill shallows are now part of a private house and are not visible. But at Chapmansford Farm, below the viaduct, it is again in good condition. I stood there with Plunket Greene's photograph and it was unchanged.

Mr John Gauntlet of Apsley Estates, who have this water, told me that in 1990 the syndicate caught 170 fish, of which 100 were wild, including one wild five pounder (2.3 kg). In Plunket Greene's day, the whole river was owned by Lord Portsmouth. The family sold up and left in 1952 and now it is split up among several owners – hence the unevenness of the upkeep.

Above the viaduct, the top mile to St Mary Bourne was totally dry in December 1990. Grass and rank weeds grew in the bed of the once sparkling stream. It did dry up in 1905 – but not in December. Plunket Greene lies buried in Hurstbourne church-yard. It is good he is not here to see it.

Longparish and Peter Hawker

We return to the Test and the Longparish water. Colonel Peter Hawker, the father of English wildfowling, lived at Longparish House and kept a diary covering the years 1801 to 1833, during which he shot over 17,000 birds and killed some 12,000 fish.

Fishing was second to shooting and his methods may seem primitive. He would have used a rod of hickory or ash, with a horsehair line, casting downstream. He used two wet flies: a yellow dun for tail fly and a small red palmer for dropper. I am sure that Hawker was a skilful angler and knew how to work his flies.

Peter Hawker's descendants lived on at Longparish House (which still stands, like an anglicised French chateau) until the early years of the 20th century. Another distinguished family, the Dawnays, lived there until 1989. The estate of about 1000 acres (404.7 ha) was then sold to an entrepreneur, Mr Roger Smee, who spent £2 million on the house. He was then forced by the recession to put the estate on the market. In January 1992 it was announced that the fishing had been bought by Mr Nick Faldo, the golfer, for £750,000. The estate is still unsold.

The fishing consists of two parallel streams, giving a total of 5 miles (8 km) of fishing, which is let to six full-season rods with occasional day rods. Most of the stocking is with fingerlings, topped up with browns up to 1 lb (.45 kg) – nothing bigger. If rainbows appear, they are treated as vermin (and a good thing too).

Mr Alf Harper deliberately keeps the banks wild, to encourage wildlife and to discourage picnic parties. This is a well run, picturesque fishery, not too heavily fished.

Middleton and the Wills

The Middleton estate, owned by the Wills family (of cigarette fame) consists of about 4,000 acres (1618 ha) with some 4 miles of fishing. There is the main river, divided into seven beats, and a carrier known as 'the half water' because the far bank belongs to the Army. The main river, which provides the best fishing, is let to full season rods, while the half water is let to rods who have one named day a week. The half water is no more than a few yards wide: too narrow, in my opinion, to have divided ownership. The Army, I am told, fish their bank hard. It must be irritating to come down to fish and find another fisherman already occupying the river from the opposite bank.

The estate is divided by the busy A303 dual carriageway which runs from London to Andover and on to Exeter. Most of the fishing – five beats – is to the north of the road, but two are to the south. It is all very pretty, but the part south of the road, with its rippling shallows, is quite enchanting.

In the last two years, major work has been done to improve the flow by narrowing the river (see diagram). This has markedly improved the whole fishery, by causing the mud to be carried away and encouraging the growth of ranunculus.

There is an unusual fishing hut on the home beat. It has a ground floor and a first floor, giving a good view of the river, and is circular with a conical thatched roof topped by a flagpole. In the

**HOW TO IMPROVE A FISHERY BY
NARROWING THE RIVER**

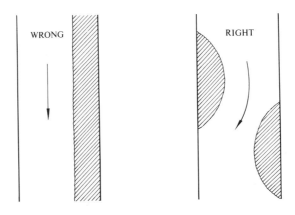

WRONG

RIGHT

days of Captain Andrew Wills' grandfather, the keeper was required to fly a flag – visible from the house, which is why the hut was built so high – to indicate that the fish were rising.

On the day I walked the river with Jeff Smith, the keeper, there was a Frenchman fishing for winter grayling. When I wished him *bonne chance*, he replied: 'Never say that to a French angler, monsieur. It brings only disaster. Better say *merde*.'

This is a splendid fishery on which considerable sums of money have been sensibly spent. The home beat, where day tickets are sometimes available, is heavily stocked and heavily fished, but the rest are lightly fished. Only browns are stocked, up to 2 lb (.9 kg). There are plenty of wild fish.

The fishing hut on the Middleton water of the upper Test, owned by the Wills family. The present owner's grandfather required the keeper to fly a flag from the roof to indicate that the fish were rising.

Wherwell

This fishery, of some 5 miles (8 km) including carriers, is similar to Longparish and Middleton above, and is run in a similar way with season rods, and some day tickets on the home beat (if not required by the owner). The river is stocked three times a season – much better than on some of the lower fisheries, where they stock every fortnight.

The keeper, Mr Bill Hawkins, buys 2,000 fry each year from Mick Lunn at Stockbridge and brings them on in his own stew up to 2 lb (.9 kg). It could be said that it would provide better fishing to put the fry straight into the river and let them grow as wild fish – but of course fewer would survive.

There is a problem with blanket weed on the slower-running stretches, caused by lack of water and hot dry summers. As we go further down the river, blanket weed becomes worse. It is a horrible sight of thick fibrous mats, suffocating the ranunculus and making fishing impossible. If weather conditions do not change, the only answer is to narrow the river to increase the flow.

The Dever

The Dever, which enters the Test at Wherwell and flows from east to west, provides 10 miles (16 km) of fishing – always good and sometimes superb. No wonder it was a favourite of Halford. No wonder it still attracts some of the best of today's chalkstream fishermen. If you want to be far from the madding crowd, and far from the roar of traffic, and enjoy all the flora and fauna of the chalk streams – fish the Dever.

The Govett Estate has 2 miles (3.2 km) of the Dever, where it joins the Test, and 2 miles (3.2 km) of the Test itself. It is lovely water, only about 5 yds (4.5 m) wide, with one bank kept deliberately wild, and well looked after by two keepers. Unfortunately, it is heavily stocked and heavily fished. Despite this, there are plenty of wild fish which offer a real challenge. Mr Govett, the owner, lets season rods and occasional Day Tickets. Next is the 1½ miles (2.4 km) of the Merison fishery, also lovely, let to season rods only. Above this, the Army have 1½ miles (2.4 km) of more open water up to the Dever Springs stillwater fishery, which specialises in huge rainbows. Then comes the 2½ miles (4 km) owned by Mr David Willis, managed by James Harris of Winchester – again, quite idyllic, and not heavily fished. There are season rods and a handful of Day Tickets. Beyond this, the Sutton Scotney Angling Club have 2 miles (3.2 km), mainly for the benefit of local anglers – and very right and proper too.

Mr Mark Ferguson, who knows the river well, told me that there is no mayfly on the Dever, but plenty of iron blue, BWO, and sherry spinner, and that the grannom has reappeared. This is interesting, for many years ago the grannom in April was as big an event as the mayfly.

There is a proposal to build 5,000 houses at Micheldever, near the source. If this happens, it would be a disaster for the Dever. Its very survival as a fishery would be threatened. Local residents have set up the Dever Society to fight it.

Chilbolton and the Reverend Richard Durnford

Richard Durnford was Rector of Chilbolton in the early years of the 19th century and kept a diary. This was published in 1911 as *The Diary of a Test Fisherman 1809 – 1819*. He was one of many sporting parsons of that era, who took their fishing more seriously than their religion. For instance, of the original 13 members of the Houghton Club, three were clergymen. They had private means, lived in large rectories, and enjoyed the life of the country. Another example was Gilbert White of Selborne, the great naturalist. There are not many these days, though Oliver Kite used to speak of the Canon of Netheravon who took matins wearing waders under his cassock.

Richard Durnford, from his portrait, was a tough, burly sort of man – more like a country squire. The diaries make good reading, and show what a fine angler he was. Unlike Hawker, he fished mainly with a blow line downstream with a natural fly. This was a method which depended on a suitable wind, and he carefully recorded the strength of the wind each day. He also used the artificial fly – wet of course – fished across and down. Usually he used a single fly, except on windy days when he added a dropper, which he kept on top of the water so that he knew

THE RIVERS OF HAMPSHIRE

where his tail fly was and did not miss the takes. He knew very well what he was doing. He did not kill on anything like the same scale as Hawker, but got some large bags at times both on the natural and artificial.

He saw nothing wrong in cross-line fishing. This involved two anglers stretching a line across the river and dapping a fly, hanging a few inches below, on the water. It must have been deadly on the wider stretches for fish in midstream, because it obviated the problem of drag. There is no record of the method ever being used by the Houghton Club. Perhaps it was too deadly.

The Chilbolton fishery today is owned by the Church of England: Richard Durnford would have approved. It is leased by a syndicate of six members who only fish the 3½ miles (5.6 km) on Tuesdays and weekends. There are also what are known as two 'Commoners Rods' which belong to Chilbolton. In 1912 there was a High Court case over the ownership of the fishery. Some in Chilbolton said that it belonged to them. The case went to the House of Lords and was settled in favour of the Church.

The keeper, Mr Mike Perry, rakes the redds at the end of the season and there is good natural spawning. They top up with 300 browns during the season between 1¼ lb (.56 kg) and 3 lb (1.36 kg). There is plenty of food in the river, and stock fish survive the winter well. One fish of 6 lb (2.72 kg) was caught in 1990, which may have been wild or a stock fish which grew on. Either way, it is a tribute to the river.

There are unwelcome signs of blanket weed, but still plenty of ranunculus. Mr Perry is sad about the disappearance of frogs from the Test, as we all are. I suspect it is connected with the use of chemicals on the land.

The Anton Tributary

In *A Summer on the Test*, John Waller Hills describes the Anton from Clatford downwards as 'a deep, fast, river, in all ways like the Test itself, a resemblance unfortunately accentuated by the fact that both valleys have railways along them.' The railways disappeared in the 1960s, under the Beeching Axe – the only good thing that has happened to the valley since Hills wrote in 1924.

The Anton flows into the Test at the well-known Mayfly Inn at Testcombe, between Leckford and Chilbolton. The upper waters divide at Upper Clatford into the main river, which flows through Andover, and the Little Ann (also known as the Pillhill Brook) which flows to the village of Amport.

On the lower Anton, there are two major fisheries: the first, at the joining with the Test, is owned by Major Charles Liddell and has 2 miles (3.2 km) of the Anton and one mile (1.6 km) of the Test (one bank only). There are 28 rods who have one day a week. It is attractive and varied water, and though lower than it should be, is still in good condition. But it is heavily fished and heavily stocked. So many fish were left in the river at the end of the 1990 season, that the keeper has found it necessary to feed them daily with pellets through the winter.

Above this, is 1½ miles (2.4 km) owned by Major Charles' brother Adrian, which is fished by ten rods also on a one day a week basis. It is indeed a big river here, deep and fast, reminding me of some parts of the Wiltshire Avon. It is also heavily stocked. Above Goodworth Clatford, the river is in small stretches of a few hundred yards.

Some keepers on the Test complain of 'the muck that comes down the Anton from Andover'. I did not see much evidence of this on my visit, but the presence of a large and expanding industrial town like Andover at its headwaters bodes ill for the future of the Anton. There is a fish farm producing table trout on the Little Ann, where in 1901 Hills caught eleven brace and had a magnificent day, and said that the water was 'unimaginably pure'. A few fish are still taken on the Little Ann, but the great days have vanished.

Leckford

The Leckford Estate of 4,000 acres (1618 ha), including 11 miles (17.7 km) of fishing on the Test and carriers, belongs to the John Lewis Partnership – the huge retail business which operates department stores over the United Kingdom as well as the Waitrose supermarket chain. The estate was acquired between 1929 and 1946 by John Spedan Lewis, founder of the Partnership, and was his home until his death in 1963. In his Will, he left it to the Partnership. It is now a large commercial farming enterprise. The house is a country club for the Partners – that is, all the employees – offering tennis, croquet, swimming, golf, and shooting as well as the fishing.

This is divided into 15 beats, five of which are reserved for Partners while ten are let to season rods mainly who have half a week each. There are occasional day tickets from the Estate Office. The fishery is run on business-like lines, with a Head Keeper and three under keepers and its own hatchery. Rainbows are stocked up to 6 lb (2.72 kg), but the average is 2 lb (.9 kg) and browns are in the majority. By the time it reaches Leckford the Test has received the waters of the Bourne, the Dever, and the Anton. It has become a big river, losing the intimacy of the upper waters. Some beats are attractive, but some are canal-like. I have fished Leckford as a guest on several occasions and have enjoyed it: but I could do without those large rainbows. Still, I must be in a minority, for it is popular with a long waiting list.

From Stockbridge to Romsey

Stockbridge is a large village divided down the middle by the A30, which runs from London to the south west. When you cross it, you take your life in your hands. One day, there will be a by-pass, and then life in Stockbridge will become pleasant again. The village has become a centre for the antique trade. On the south side, above the Town Hall, is a trout weather vane designed by Sir Francis Chantry, the Victorian artist and member of the Houghton Club. Nearby is a branch of Orvis, selling all that the chalk stream angler requires. In the centre of the village, on the north side is the Grosvenor Hotel, with its portico, home of the Houghton Club.

The Houghton Club

Founded in 1822, the Houghton Club is the oldest fishing club in England. Its 24 members have 15 miles (24.1 km) of the Test, from Leckford down to Bossington. Since 1887, when William

Ted Hughes, Poet Laureate and keen fisherman, on the upper Test.

Lunn was appointed Head Keeper the fishing has been maintained by a Lunn. William was followed by his son Alf, who was followed by his son Mick. With five under keepers, the waters are kept and stocked – with browns and rainbows from their own fish farm – to a very high standard.

It would seem extraordinary, in some parts of the English-speaking world, that 24 wealthy men should be able to reserve, for their exclusive use, 15 miles (24.1 km) of the most famous river in England. Democratic it is not. Yet democracy, the great catchword of our times, is not a universal panacea. Applied to the Test, the scene would be a rush like Harrods on the opening day of the sales and soon there would be nothing left. The members are envied, but also respected for the fact that they have always seen that the river is well cared for.

The Houghton Club is a fellowship of friends, who consider their times together in the club room above the Grosvenor Hotel portico to be as important as their fishing. The twelve leather-bound Journals of the Club abound with wit, comic verse, humorous drawings by artists like Chantry, Landseer, and Turner, as well as meticulous records of fish caught. My own favourite among the entries is this:

10 May 1940. Germany today invaded Holland and Belgium. Mr Neville Chamberlain resigned and Mr Winston Churchill became PM. A warm bright day with a poor rise. Few fish moving.

The three generations of Lunns have made major contributions to the art of fly dressing and river management. William devised some forty dry flies, many of which are still in widespread use. Few would go to the Test today without a Lunns Particular, or a Caperer, or a Houghton Ruby. Alf's contribution was the establishment of the fish farm, which now supplies not only the Club waters, but most of the other Test fisheries as well.

Mick Lunn saved the upper Test from the ravages of the disease UDN in the sixties, a tale which is told in his book *A Particular Lunn*, published in 1990, and a book which has already found its way on to many shelves. It is full of Mick's sunny temperament, like Izaak Walton himself, and Mick knows more about fly fishing than Izaak ever did!

Mick Lunn, Head Keeper of the Houghton Club. His grandfather William invented the Lunn's Particular, and 40 other dry flies, many of which are still popular. Mick retired in 1991.

It is widely believed that F. M. Halford was a member of the Club, but this was not so. The misunderstanding arose because Halford wrote in his autobiography: 'In 1877, I joined the Houghton Fly Fishing Club.' The Journal makes clear what happened. In 1874, it states, they lost three miles of water below Stockbridge. 'This water was let to 20 gentlemen who adopted the title of the Houghton Fly Fishing Club.' Halford was one of

Frederick M. Halford (1844–1914), the most influential of all chalk stream writers, whose reputation is now restored.

The River Test at Leckford, Hampshire

Concealment is all-important on the chalk streams

A fish rising on the Dun, a tributary of the Test *(left)*

Trying for a spring salmon in early March on the River Avon
at Ringwood, Hampshire, below the old main-road bridge

Fishing the River Wylye at Chilhampton Farm, Wilton, Wiltshire *(left)*

The River Allen, Dorset, below Stanbridge Mill

John Goddard fishing the Wilderness water of the Kennet
below Hungerford, Berkshire

John Roberts pulling in a trout on the Driffield West Beck, Yorkshire *(right)*

Fishing the dry fly on the Driffield West Beck at Wansford, Yorkshire the twenty, as was Francis Francis, G. S. Marryat, and William Senior. Halford took rooms at Houghton Mill, and this was where the serious work was done. I do not think Halford would have fitted in at the Houghton Club. Certainly the members took their fishing seriously, but not the extent of spending their evenings dissecting the blue-winged olive.

In 1893, the Club managed to regain their waters below Stockbridge, and the Houghton Fly Fishing Club ceased to exist. But by then Halford's two great works, which changed the whole nature of dry fly fishing, had been published.

F. M. Halford on the Test

Let us picture Halford and his friends in those years. Halford had taken rooms at Houghton Mill for the season, and from there they would go forth, on foot probably, and start fishing. Halford and Marryat would be kneeling over a fish, carrying out an autopsy and examining the stomach contents. This was a messy business, made unnecessary later by Skues' use of the marrow spoon. They would catch flies, with a fine mesh net, and put them in a bottle. They would wade out, and examine weed for larvae or nymphs.

In the evening, with fly-tying vice, microscope, and notebook, they examined and dissected and recorded. Halford kept copious and meticulous notebooks. Out of all this came dry flies which, for the first time, would float for more than a few seconds. They used non-water absorbing quill bodies, stiff hackles, and split wings to make the fly ride better. They classified their new patterns under the various headings of the natural flies.

They had some advantages. Three inventions had just appeared – the eyed hook, which made it easy to change flies, the silk line, which unlike horsehair did not sag or become waterlogged, and the split cane rod, which made it possible to cast upstream against the wind. Halford put it all together into a new, and revolutionary, doctrine of dry fly fishing.

In the 1990 reprint of Halford's *Dry Fly Fishing in Theory and Practice* Dermot Wilson writes in a Preface: 'Its most striking feature is its extraordinary relevance today. From cover to cover it is choc-a-bloc with essential information and practical suggestions, some of them far from widely known, yet nearly all of them as valid and helpful in this day and age as they were a hundred years ago.'

Halford has been heavily criticised as 'the fastidious high priest of the dry fly' whose belief in exact imitation, involving the angler carrying a hundred patterns, is ridiculed. When he wrote *Dry Fly Fishing*, at the age of forty-four, he was less dogmatic than is popularly supposed. He praised the skill of the wet-fly fisherman. He wrote that 'in casting to an uneducated fish the selection of fly is of far less importance, and accuracy and delicacy of far greater importance'. He goes on to say that the educated fish is more suspicious of the artificial, and then selection is crucial. This is modern orthodox doctrine. Why has he been so heavily criticised?

As he grew older, he certainly became somewhat rigid in his views. Most of us do! In his youth, he had been an all-round angler but in old age the dry fly had become an obsession. But when *Dry Fly Fishing* was published in 1889, its impact was so great that a whole cult of dry fly fishing grew up. Some of these disciples carried the doctrine to absurd lengths. They – not Halford himself – were the dry fly snobs.

Halford corresponded with Theodore Gordon in the United States, and sent over some of his flies. Gordon was impressed, and adapted Halford's principles for American conditions. If Gordon is the father of American fly dressing, then Halford is the grandfather.

I have been fortunate to have had long discussions with Mr John Halford, F.M.Halford's great grandson, and to have seen his notebooks and many other papers. The obituaries were by no means formal eulogies. They came from people in many walks of life, and showed that he was held in genuine affection – and was, in fact, far from the crusty, pompous, blinkered old buffer of popular legend. He was, for example, a great tease. He was fond of children, and they liked him.

When he lost the water below Stockbridge, he obtained a long lease on a mile of the Oakley Stream at Mottisfont, a few miles down. He took a cottage at Dunbridge for the season, employed as keeper Bob Coxon (who lived until 1989), and invited his friends down to fish.

At the end of the season he always gave a dinner at the Mottisfont Parish Hall for all those who had helped with the fishing. As many as fifty attended. He erected a comfortable fishing hut on the Oakley Stream which still stands. It was his habit to go to warmer climes in the winter, and after Christmas 1913, he went to Tunis with his son Cecil. On the return journey by sea, having been in perfect health, he suddenly caught pneumonia and was dead in two days. The date was 5 March 1914 and he was in his seventieth year.

Marsh Court

The Marsh Court fishery has 2½ miles (4 km) below Stockbridge, most of it on a carrier, with some on the main river shared with the Houghton Club. The Test is a big river here, too wide to cast across, and I would prefer the carrier. Season rods are let by Roxtons of Hungerford on a one-day-a-week basis, and it is stocked with browns averaging 2 lb (.9 kg) with a few rainbows. As the Houghton Club also stock rainbows, it would be pointless not to do so.

Marsh Court has always been a celebrated Test fishery. The house was built by Lutyens in the early years of this century, and is of major architectural importance. The original owner was Mr Herbert Johnson, a city financier who made and lost three fortunes during the building, which stretched over ten years. The estate was bought in 1948 by Sir Harold Bowden (of Raleigh Industries and Bowden cables), who decided the house was too big, let it as a school, and built himself a smaller house. After Sir Harold's death, the fishery was run by his widow, Valerie, Lady Bowden, another of the Test's eccentric and formidable ladies.

The school closed in 1987, since when Marsh Court has been on the market. Lutyens built the walls of chalk, in the traditional way, but this requires a high standard of maintenance. If water is allowed to penetrate, deterioration is rapid. Empty for three years, the house today is a sorry sight of dilapidation and neglect. Soon it will be beyond repair, unless the Lutyens Society can raise the funds to save it.

Marsh Court, near Stockbridge on the Test. The house was built by Lutyens using the local material – chalk. It has been empty for three years and is suffering from lack of maintenance.

Bossington

Below the Houghton Club and Marsh Court water, we come to the Bossington fishery, owned by the Fairey estate. It has 4 miles (6.43 km) of water, divided into eight beats and season rods fish on a rota system, every fourth day. One beat is kept in hand, and day tickets are sometimes available. The bag for 1990 was over 2000 trout, about half browns and half rainbows. It is heavily fished, but there is a waiting list.

Sir Richard Fairey, who bought the estate, died in 1956. He was a pioneer aircraft manufacturer, whose most famous plane was the Fairey Swordfish, which flew from an aircraft carrier to torpedo and disable the Bismarck. In Sir Richard's day, the fishing was kept for his family and guests. Nowadays, succeeded by his son, Mr John Fairey, the fishing, like the rest of the estate, has to pay its way.

The Fairey estate also owns two beats on the Wallop Brook, once a delightful little stream but now ruined by water abstraction near the source. In 1989 and 1990, it was unfishable. ★

Compton

This fishery is in many ways similar to Bossington, even to the ownership. Until very recently, the owner was another aircraft pioneer, Sir Thomas Sopwith, whose factories had built the Hawker Hurricane for the Battle of Britain. Sir Thomas began to let rods about 1976. Season rods can fish every day if they wish. The water is stocked every fortnight with 50 per cent browns (average 2½ lb/1.1 kg) and 50 per cent rainbows (up to 5 lb/2.3 kg).

There are the usual problems with reduced flow, blanket weed, and the use of pesticide sprays on the meadows. It is an open fishery, and wind could be troublesome. Still fly life remains good, with plentiful mayfly, iron blue, and sedges.

After Sir Thomas's death, at the age of 101, in 1989, the estate was sold to a group of Chinese gentlemen from Hong Kong. There were plans to convert the house into a hotel and construct a golf course: but due to the recession, all is at the moment in abeyance.

★ Abstraction was less in 1991, and it was fishable again.

John Waller Hills

Hills fished the Oakley Stream at Mottisfont in the twenties, where Halford had fished in the 1890s, and must have eaten his sandwiches in the hut which Halford put up, and which still stands. But he knew the chalk streams very well: in *A Summer on the Test* he mentions fishing at Longparish, on the Bourne and Dever, at Leckford, Kimbridge, and on the Houghton Club water, where he was a member from 1925–30. He also fished the Itchen – once as a guest of Skues – the Yorkshire Driffield, the Kennet, the Otter in Devon, and the Derbyshire Wye.

During these years he was a Conservative MP, and for a time was Financial Secretary to the Treasury and a Privy Councillor. How did he find the time? Those were more leisured days. He died in 1938.

There are fishermen who write, and there are writers who fish. Hills was unique in being both. He knew his entomology, and varied his tactics according to the season, the time of day, and the weather. He also had time to stand and stare, as this passage shows:

> And oh, the joy in the evening, when the sun has set and the hot wind has dropped, and a grateful coolness rises from the earth, and moths like moving shadows are feeding at the river grasses, and nightjars are churring in the wood, and the meadow darkens under the opal twilight – oh, the joy and the confidence of looping on a stronger cast.

Nowadays, with our high-quality nylon leaders, we do not have his problems with gut, but this apart his advice on fishing methods is as sound now as it was then. Although he was always a dry fly man, he was receptive to Skues' teachings on the nymph, and was feeling his way to the use of the sunk nymph, a technique later to be brought to fruition by Sawyer on the Avon (see pages 91–94).

In some ways he was ahead of his time. He wrote that if trout were to be stocked, it should be done with fish from that particular river, not 'trout of alien race, bred in foreign surroundings'. He tells how Halford and his friends stocked the Ramsbury water on the Kennet with 'barbarians from High Wycombe' with the result that the fishing went from bad to worse. Only recently has that view been widely accepted.

Near the end of *A Summer on the Test* he writes: 'I have made no wonderful discoveries. What I have learnt, very painfully, has been invented by others. So I propound no theory and preach no creed.' Like Plunket Greene, but in a more restrained, English, way, he could communicate the joy of fishing the chalk streams seventy years ago. His place in history is secure.

Mottisfont

The National Trust own 1½ miles (2.4 km) of the main river at Mottisfont. They lease it to Sir Owen Aisher of Marley Tiles who does not let rods. It includes the Oakley Stream where Halford and J. W. Hills fished. Mottisfont has an Abbey – also National Trust – with a well-known rose garden showing old English roses. It is a glorious sight in June.

Halford's hut on the Oakley Stream near Mottisfont on the Test. J. W. Hills also fished here. The water now belongs to Mr Owen Aisher.

Kimbridge

This is a major fishery with 5½ miles (8.8 km) of fishing (including a mile (1.6 km) of the Dun) and is let to season rods only who are allowed 30 days, to be taken at their choice. The fishery is owned by Mr Arthur Humbert, who farms the land and also owns a large fish farm on the Test. In 1988, Ready Mixed Concrete plc made a planning application to extract gravel and sand from a field to the west of the river near Dunbridge, carry it a mile across the valley – and over the river – to another field by the side of the main A3057 Romsey – Stockbridge road, there to be dumped and picked up by lorries and taken to building sites. It involved the construction of a conveyor belt a mile long, across the valley and over the river. There was intense local – and national – opposition, which resulted in a full-scale Local Inquiry. When this decided in favour of the proposal, there was a feeling of despair.

Now, in the summer of 1991, extraction is in full swing. The conveyor belt runs silently on rubber wheels, is about 3 ft (1 m) high and is screened by grass banks. Where it crosses the river it is boxed in and is no more unsightly than a small bridge. The environment has not been harmed. The protesters, of whom I was one, were wrong. It was a lot of unnecessary fuss.

The Dun Tributary

The Dun, which enters the Test at Kimbridge, rises about five miles (8 km) to the west, at Clarendon. It flows through the villages of West Dean, East Dean, Lockerley, and Dunbridge. The first (bottom) mile, at Kimbridge is part of Mr Humbert's fishery. Then comes a mile or so owned by Mr McDonald Hall of Lockerley and another stretch owned (partly leased) by the Nat West Bank Fishing Club. After some small stretches in private hands, there is about three-quarters of a mile owned by Mr Peter Redshaw of Holbury Mill Farm. Mr Wilmot of East Dean has some water, but above that the river tends to dry up in the summer. The Dun is a lovely, if variable, river. William Lunn came to it in the 1890s to collect mayfly larvae for the Houghton Club. I have seen excellent mayfly in parts, though it has

The Test at Kimbridge.

completely disappeared from others. Likewise, there are good
hatches of iron blue and olives in the faster running parts, but in
other places the flow is too sluggish to support ranunculus and
hence there is a lack of fly. Nevertheless, the Dun is a beautiful,
unspoilt, stream, and it has its devotees, among whom I am
proud to be included.

A botanically-minded wife of a fishing friend recorded the
following flora on the Dun in June 1991: Herb Robert, Lesser
Stitchwort, Mouse Ear Chickweed, Yellow Archangel, Ground
Ivy, Bugle, Germander Speedwell, Buttercup. Jack-by-the-
Hedge, Creeping Thistle, Forget-me-not, Woodaven, Ragged
Robin, Hedge Parsley, Daisy, Kingcups, Brooklime, Water
Celery, Wild Raspberry.

Timsbury

Below Kimbridge on the main river is the Timsbury water of 3 miles (4.8 km), owned by Mr Oppenheim and fished by a syndicate of 28 members who fish on a rotation system. It is heavily fished, for mixed browns and rainbows. The Test suffers here from silt, and is often cloudy, and there is the ubiquitous blanket weed.

Greatbridge

Here there are 1¾miles (2.7 km) owned by Mr Christopher Saunders Davies, who also has a large commercial fish farm. He said to me: 'To make money out of the river would require severe fishing pressure which I think would be bad for the river, so we fish it lightly and we do not make money out of it. We only have a part-time keeper.'

To summarise, although there is an attempt in places, by introducing fry, to produce semi-wild fish, it is largely true that the Test from Stockbridge to Romsey is nothing more than a put-and-take fishery. The valley itself keeps its charm. The flow is reduced, but the flow of anglers willing to pay to fish here is undiminished.

From Romsey to the Sea

Romsey (pop 15,000) is a pleasant Hampshire town, famous for its Abbey and Broadlands (of which more later). Remarkably, the town owns a quarter mile (.4 km) of the Test, where it flows through the town park, and day tickets can be bought from Test Valley District Council in the town for as little as £15 in 1991. A few years ago, when salmon were plentiful, tickets were hard to come by – but those days are gone. No salmon were taken in 1990.

In the town, at Abbey Mill, is an interesting fishery owned by Mr David Steuart. It is only half a mile (.8 km), but within that area it is varied, with a deep slow stretch, a fine weir pool, and good spawning shallows. Up to 1986, this little fishery produced

The late Lt. Col. Gibson Bishop with a 36½ lb (16.6 kg) salmon taken on a
yellow belly minnow, *c.* 1966, at the Royalty Fishery on the Hampshire Avon.

an average of 60 salmon a year – one year it produced 77. In 1990 the tally was six. Walking the river with Mr Steuart in December 1990, we saw about half a dozen spawning pairs, where there used to be 60. This sorry tale is repeated as we go down the river.

Broadlands

Broadlands, through which 5½ miles (8.8 km) of the Test runs, was the home of Lord Louis Mountbatten and is now the home of his grandson, Lord Romsey. The house, which is open to the public from Easter to October, contains fascinating memorabilia of Lord Louis' glittering career. Here, the river justifies the word 'stately'. It has a certain grandeur as it meanders through the meadows, dotted here and there with magnificent oaks and beeches.

In the sixties, when I fished there with that well-known fisherman Col. Gibson Bishop (who always took at least one 18 lb (8.2 kg) springer), Broadlands produced 350 salmon a year. There were happy gatherings in the fishing hut with Bernard Aldrich, the keeper. The decline set in in the late seventies, and the score in 1990 was six. A few years ago, it was decided to turn over part of the fishery to stocked trout. Now there are six beats – three salmon, and three trout (browns only). The fishing is widely advertised in the angling press, with a fishing package including a stay at Lee Park Lodge on the estate, and day tickets are available. Twenty years ago, it was almost impossible to obtain a rod at Broadlands. There was a waiting list of many years. Now there are day tickets!

Nursling

Below Broadlands lies the 6 miles (9.6 km) of the Nursling fishery, in two parallel streams known as the Main River and the Little Test, with the productive Drawing Room Pool. In the distance is Southampton and the Fawley oil refinery.

The landscape is full of industrial estates. Pylons march across the meadows. We are a long way here from the villages of the upper Test, with their rural peace. We are in another world.

And yet the Nursling fishery is not without charm. Trees hide much of the ugliness, and I can understand its popularity with the 24 rods who fish it. The keeper, Vic Foot, gives it his devoted care. It used to produce 500 salmon a year. In 1990 it produced 95 – which for these days is good.

The final fishery is Testwood, which runs from Nursling down to the mouth at Totton. Again, this is a fishery which manages to remain attractive amid squalor. It is owned by the Barker Mills Estate at Marchwood, Southampton. The decline here has been less. An average year produced 300 salmon, and in 1988 it produced 327: in 1990, 160.

Conclusion

It would be unjustified to end the story of the Test on a note of unrelieved gloom. The National Rivers Authority are spending a good deal of time and money on research into the decline of the salmon, including tracking with fish counters and radio transmitters in selected fish. Is the decline due to conditions in the river or out at sea? It may be a mixture of both. The Test has many powerful friends. We must hope for wet winters, to see whether the droughts of 1989 and 1990 were a major cause of the decline.

As regards the trout fisheries, there is one striking fact. Talking to people up and down the river, one hears of decline: of lack of water, of blanket weed, of lack of ranunculus, of turbidity, of pollution. And yet, if you inquire what the 1990 season was like, the answer is always 'Despite everything, we had a good season'. Despite it all, and despite over-stocking and over-fishing in some places, there is still first class dry fly fishing to be found on some parts of the Test.

—————— THE MEON ——————

The Meon, the most easterly of the Hampshire chalk streams, flows through the same sort of countryside as the Itchen – a mellowed and matured landscape, where human handiwork is more evident that it is in Wiltshire and Dorset. Through parks dotted with stately oaks and cedars, there are glimpses of ivy-clad country homes, built in more civilized centuries than this one.

The Meon is much smaller than the Itchen, faster flowing and very clear. The best parts present a real challenge to fishermen, for the fish are easily 'spooked'. It is varied, with gravel shallows, deep pools, open meadows, and closely wooded stretches. Unfortunately, much of it has become unfishable. Of the total course of 15 miles (29.1 km) from East Meon down to the Solent at Stubbington, only the middle five miles (8 km) from Warnford to Wickham remain in good condition. The top five miles (8 km) are dry, due to over abstraction, and the bottom part is too dirty, due to a population explosion in recent years at Fareham.

How long the present fishing will remain, no one knows. In 1990, fishing had to stop in July and August because the water was too low. The cause of the trouble is over abstraction at Soberton Mill, by the Portsmouth Water Co. This is exactly the sort of place, half-way up the river, where abstraction should never be allowed. There is also heavy abstraction at Titchfield, lower down, which does not harm the trout fishing, but has effectively ended the run of migratory salmon and sea trout. As there is little current, few fish run up to spawn. Sea trout are still caught occasionally by coarse anglers near the mouth. And as the bottom of the river runs through built up areas, it is heavily poached.

The first fishery of note is Mr J. M. Horne's water between Meonstoke and Droxford where there is a syndicate and also day tickets. Below this, the Portsmouth Services Fly Fishing Association have four miles (6.4 km) down to Wickham. They also have two miles (3.2 km) of the Itchen below Winchester.

They have 140 members (including 11 retired Admirals!) of whom 15 can fish each day. In their top beats, which are the best, they are trying to introduce a catch-and-release policy, so as to make it less of a frequently stocked put-and-take fishery. I hope they succeed, for the Meon is infinitely worth preserving. One young member said to me: 'Despite it all, the Meon is still a lovely little river.' Dick Stacey, the Hon. Sec, commented: 'The young ones say that. They do not remember what it was like twenty years ago, with wild fish and plenty of water.'

There is one other trout fishery, on about a mile and a half (2.4 km) of a rather sluggish carrier between Segensworth and Titchfield Mill, which is run by the Park Gate branch of the Royal British Legion. In the sixties, this was an outstanding sea trout water, but now the sea trout have almost disappeared. It is believed that some still run up after the end of the season. In the marshy country where the Meon enters the Solent, the local authority purchased the land some years ago to create a bird sanctuary. Anglers and wildfowlers had to leave. There is nothing wrong in that, except that they paid a vastly inflated price for it, and the cormorants have become a menace.

One name which will always be associated with the Meon is that of the late Richard Seymour. He was Bursar of a school in Portsmouth, a good sea trout angler, and river management was his passion. In the seventies he found the Meon overgrown and neglected. Gathering volunteers from the boys, and infecting them with his own enthusiasm, he set to work clearing the river, repairing the banks, and putting it back in good order. Southern Television made a popular film of his work, with the commentator Martin Muncaster. He died in 1983, at the age of 61, of a heart attack, on the banks of the river he loved.

THE UPPER AVON
and Wiltshire Bourne

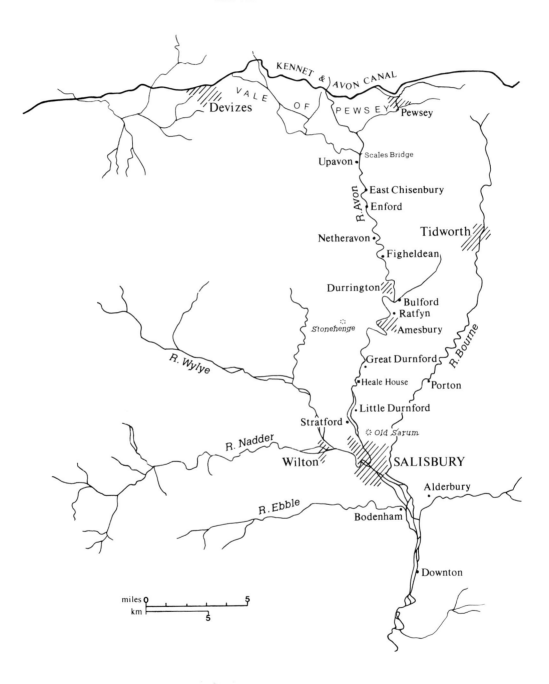

3

THE RIVERS OF
WILTSHIRE

Avon
including the Bourne and the Ebble

Nadder

Wylye

THE AVON

Superficially, the Avon suffers in comparison with the Test and the Itchen. It lacks their glamour. It has no Halford, no Grey, no John Waller Hills, no Houghton Club. But it has its share of the literary heritage: Frank Sawyer and Oliver Kite, though they belong to our own times, are already legends and have their place in fly fishing history.

In the quality of fishing it offers, it compares well. Maybe the dry fly fishing between the source and Salisbury is slightly inferior to the best of the Itchen, but below Salisbury both the coarse fishing and the salmon fishing in the lower reaches are undoubtedly superior. Nor is its setting of rolling chalk downs and pretty thatched villages in any way inferior. I have been surprised how many people, when asked to name the most beautiful spot in the chalk streams, plump for Gunville Hatches, below the village of Figheldean.

The Avon rises in the Vale of Pewsey. Two headwater streams, known as the East and West Avon, unite at Upavon, where the main river begins. The West Avon rises in greensand and is unlike a chalk stream – just a brown, featureless ditch. The East Avon is more like a chalk stream, though it too is marginally greensand.

At this point, we must briefly digress into geology. Chalk consists of the remains of marine creatures and is 97 per cent pure. Limestone is also basically chalk, but is much less pure. The chalk was formed some 200 million years ago, when the sea covered much – but not all – of southern England. Parts which were not covered, like the Vale of Pewsey, are not chalk, but greensand. The sea receded over many millions of years, but the final split of England from the continent of Europe, and the formation of the southern chalk streams, only dates from about 25,000 years ago.

Because of its greensand beginnings, the Avon is thus not a true chalk stream. After heavy rain, it can take two or three days to clear, whereas a true chalk stream will clear in hours. Also, the water is less alkaline and therefore food for fish is not so abundant. But as the river winds its way down the valley, it is augmented by numberless chalk springs, and flows through chalk, and shows the typical characteristics of a chalk stream.

Just below the village of Upavon is the first fishery of significance – the three miles (4.8 km) of the East Chisenbury Fishing Syndicate. The setting of high, steep, chalk downs through which the river runs is unusual – quite different from Hampshire – and gives this fishery a charm all its own. The fishery was little known until 1981, when the late Dick Pease published *River Keeper* which told of his years of caring for the fishery. Now the river is in the equally devoted care of his successor, Brigadier Bill Bruce-Jones.

Because of the steepness of the surrounding hills, many of which are ploughed, the fishery is vulnerable to agricultural run-off, and there are two fish farms on the East Avon. There is little natural spawning, and the practice has been to stock with about 1000 browns of around 1 lb (.45 kg). Up to a couple of years ago, everything went on more or less happily, but then a dispute arose with a local resident who has the legal right to control hatches about half-way down the fishery. He has diverted water into his garden, as he is legally entitled to do, but this has caused a deterioration in the fishing. The situation at the end of 1991 is that fishing is likely to cease altogether and the syndicate may disband. This would be a tragedy.

The Services Water

Below Chisenbury we come to the Services Dry Fly Fishing Association water of 6½ miles (10.4 km), from Enford down to Bulford. It has 100 members from all ranks of the Services: at present 60 per cent are serving and 40 per cent retired. Priority is given to those serving. In theory, all, from Privates to Field Marshals, are equal by the riverside.

Frank Sawyer (1906–80) was Head Keeper of the Services Water for 52 years, and is acknowledged as one of the great figures of the chalk streams, who through his books *Keeper of the Stream* (1952) and *Nymphs and the Trout* (1958, revised 1970) made a permanent contribution to the art of chalk stream fishing. I knew him well for twenty years, and have already written of his life and achievements (see Bibliography). Here, I will only

Frank Sawyer (1906–1980), who was Head Keeper of the Army fishing on the upper Avon. He devised the Pheasant Tail Nymph – the most successful artificial ever invented and now used all over the world.

attempt to summarise his work, and to indicate the sort of man he was.

He will always be associated with the sunk, weighted, nymph. Because of his work as a river keeper, he spent much time actually in the river. This, together with exceptional underwater vision, enabled him to observe fish feeding on nymphs in mid water. A factor which will have helped him is the way in which the river in places clings tightly to the steep downs, shutting out reflected light and making it easier to see into the water. Sawyer was interested in what he called the 'active nymph', swimming about in mid water before it ascended to the surface, there to cast its shuck and emerge as a winged insect. Skues, it will be remembered, concentrated his attention on the nymph in this final stage, which Sawyer called the 'ready to hatch' nymph. Sawyer observed that the active nymph formed a major part of the fish's diet, and he set himself to devise artificials to imitate them. The result was the Pheasant Tail nymph, to imitate the olives, and the Grey Goose to imitate the pale wateries.

The Pheasant Tail nymph is, without doubt, the most successful artificial ever invented. It is used all over the world, both in rivers and stillwaters. And yet, what could be more simple? All it consists of is a few pheasant tail fibres and some fine copper wire. Anyone can tie one after a few minutes instruction. It is, of course, the profound thought behind it which is the reason for its success. The Grey Goose is equally simple in construction and just as successful, but less used because olives are more common than pale wateries.

In *Nymphs and the Trout* Sawyer expounded his theories of fishing the sunk nymph, which became known as 'the Netheravon style'. Charles Ritz, who stayed with Sawyer in his cottage at Netheravon, was captivated and described it as the acme of fly fishing. Sawyer was not only a fisherman and river keeper with original ideas on the maintenance of chalk streams, but a broadcaster, a TV personality, and a naturalist. *Keeper of the Stream* has been compared (by the well-known writer T. B. Thomas) with Gilbert White's *Selborne*.

Sawyer was born at Bulford, where his grandfather had been the miller, and after marriage moved upstream to Netheravon. He lived in Court Farm House, in the main street, and opposite, in White Owl Cottage, in the late fifties and early sixties, lived Oliver Kite, who had just retired as a Major, from the regular Army. As neighbours, and keen fishermen, they soon became friends. For about six months, Kite spent almost every evening with Sawyer, absorbing the doctrine of the sunk nymph. In 1963, he published *Nymph Fishing in Practice*, which he described as a tribute to Sawyer. It was, and still is, an excellent exposition of nymph fishing: but the ideas were not his – they were Sawyer's. After the book appeared, there was an estrangement between them. Did Kite feel guilty? He ignored Sawyer, and when he died in 1968 Sawyer said: 'Now I shall never know why he behaved to me like that.'

Kite and Sawyer were opposites in almost everything. In common they had a consuming passion for fishing, a desire to uncover its mysteries, and a high degree of skill. Both could land a fly on a saucer at 20 yds (18.2 m). Both were fine entomologists and countrymen. After that, they diverged.

Kite was a large, robust man with twinkling eyes, an extrovert and a raconteur, with a quick, fertile, brain and a fluent pen. He had all the social graces. Sawyer was tall and angular, slightly stooped from physical toil, slow moving and speaking, keen eyed as a heron. His expression was severe. He could be difficult at times – wary and suspicious, shy and inhibited. But once he gave you his trust – which could take years – he was the most rewarding of friends with an unexpected sense of humour. He was transparently honest. He said what he thought, and did not take kindly to having his opinion on a fishing matter questioned.

Nothing came easily to Sawyer. Writing was never a pleasure, although he learnt to master it. Public speaking was something he never mastered, and he would get over this by inviting questions, which he could always deal with from his vast store of piscatorial knowledge. Kite had no problems with public speaking. He was clear, logical, and amusing. He could dash off an article for an angling magazine, while Sawyer had to burn the midnight oil.

Sawyer had a relentless, dogged, determination. He never gave up. Nature does not reveal her secrets easily, but Sawyer was one of those rare people with the qualities to persuade her to do so. Kite was a man of varied talents: but Sawyer had a touch of genius.

The Services take about 1800 fish (browns only) a season. They stock twice yearly with takeable fish of 11 in. (27.9 cm). It has been found that fry no longer thrive, because the water quality has declined. The fish are reared in their own hatchery (established by Sawyer) at Haxton, near Netheravon. For twenty years, there has been no natural spawning. There are yellow irises in May, and lady smocks, and the meadows are painted gold for our delight: but the valley is far from well.

At Durrington, about a mile (1.6 km) upstream of Bulford,

one bank is owned by the Avon Springs stillwater fishery. Their main business is to operate two lakes stocked with rainbows, but they also own some three quarters of a mile (1.2 km) of river, which they stock with browns up to 2 lb (.9 kg). There are also plenty of grayling. Day tickets are available for the river at a most reasonable price. There is good mayfly and other small flies, and I have seen splendid sedge hatches on a summer evening. For those new to the chalk streams, who would like to try it out without committing themselves, this is an ideal way to start. (For details see Price Guide on page 175).

Salisbury and District Angling Club

Below Bulford, as we approach the northern outskirts of Amesbury, we come to the first of the waters belonging to the Salisbury and District Angling Club. This is at Ratfyn, where they have a mile of river and a small lake stocked with rainbows.

By any standards, this is a remarkable club. It began in 1941 with six members fishing a small stretch of the Bourne on the edge of Salisbury with a small lake nearby. Now, 50 years later, they have 25 miles (40.2 km) of fishing and five lakes, and 1400 members of whom sixty per cent are game fishers and forty per cent coarse fishers. About ten miles (16 km) of rivers (Avon, Wylye, Nadder and Bourne) are chalk stream, dry fly water. Over their history, the balance between game and coarse has varied. Sometimes one has predominated, sometimes the other. But the club has always been keen to be known as a mixed fishing club, and to encourage the all-rounder.

How is it that they have been so successful? There have been two moving spirits – Mr John Eadie and Mr Gordon Topp, both Salisbury men. They have been enterprising: for instance, in the early seventies, they bought the freehold fishing rights to 2 miles (3.2 km) of the Avon at West Amesbury for £12,000 – including a grant of £6000 from the Sports Council. It seemed risky at the time, but it has turned out a bargain.

The Club has water on the Avon above Salisbury as follows: Ratfyn (2 miles/3.2 km) West Amesbury (2 miles/3.2 km) Little Durnford (2 miles/3.2 km) and Stratford including the river within the City (2½ miles/4 km). The first three fisheries are purely game, but Stratford is mixed. In May, when the coarse fishers are in their close season, the gamefishers enjoy the mayfly until 16 June, when the coarse season starts.

The large membership gives a cash flow which enables the Club to employ a full-time keeper and to own a weed-cutting boat, to operate stew ponds and to stock regularly. It is a well-run club, but, people ask, are the waters impossibly crowded? One long-time member told me that he had never failed to find a place to fish. The choice was so wide, if one stretch was full, there was always another available somewhere else.

When told that the subscription for 1991 is £73, and for that one can fish seven days a week, taking not more than a brace a day, people are suspicious. All that fishing for so little? There must be a catch. I can assure them there is no catch. It is simply outstanding value. With this on offer, anyone who pays £80 to fish for one day on the Test for stocked rainbows, is very foolish indeed.

From Amesbury to Salisbury

Below the Salisbury Club water at West Amesbury, there is about a mile (1.6 km) belonging to Wilsford Manor, where lived the Hon. Stephen Tennant (1906–87). Tennant was a wealthy aesthete and a talented, but not outstanding, artist and poet. He loved to entertain his friends, who included Cecil Beaton, Siegfried Sassoon, Rex Whistler, E. M. Forster, Vita Sackville West, Virginia Woolf and many others.

Tennant died in 1987, lonely and ill, with the house and gardens falling into decay around him. It was then bought by Mr Myles d'Arcy Irvine, who has restored the house and gardens to his own taste, and with the help of Mr Simon Cain, has brought the fishing back to first-class condition.

The Piscatorial Society ★

We now come to the Piscatorials' water of 3 miles (4.8 km), some of it leased from Lord Tryon of Great Durnford, where his uncle,

★ See also p 50.

THE MIDDLE AND LOWER AVON

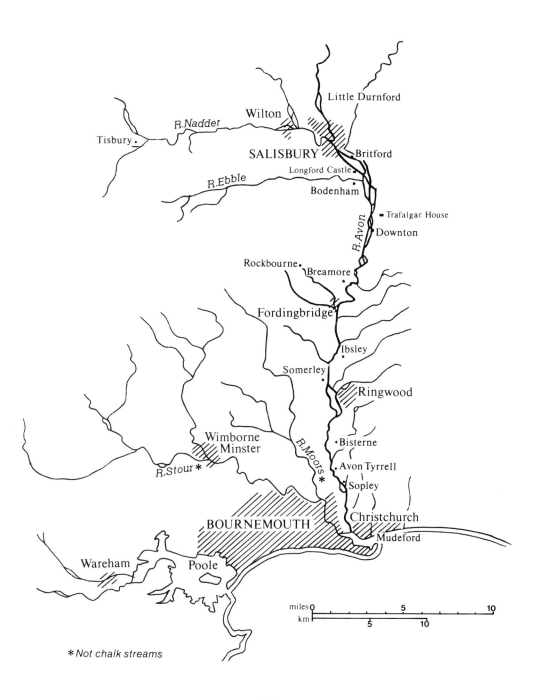

Little Durnford

Wilton

R.Nadder

Tisbury.

SALISBURY

Britford

R.Ebble

Longford Castle

Bodenham

Trafalgar House

R.Avon

Downton

Rockbourne.

Breamore

Fordingbridge

Ibsley

Somerley

Ringwood

Wimborne Minster

R.Stour *

R.Moors

Bisterne

Avon Tyrrell

Sopley

BOURNEMOUTH

Christchurch

Mudeford

Wareham

Poole

miles 0   5   10
km   5   10

*Not chalk streams

the Hon. Aylmer Tryon, also lives at Kingfisher Lodge. Aylmer has a short stretch of the river and has written delightfully about it in his book *The Quiet Waters By*.

The Avon has always been a good grayling river, from Upavon down to Salisbury. In the fifties, Frank Sawyer once removed 10,000 from the Services water alone. He invented the Killer Bug to remove grayling, and I have more than once seen him catch 60 in an afternoon. But those days are gone. Grayling have declined up and down the river. The Piscatorials no longer remove them by electric fishing. A decline in grayling is ominous, for it is the first indication that the quality of the water has decreased.

Below the Piscatorials is the 3½ miles (5.6 km) of the Heale House water, owned by Major David Rasch. It is water that I have known, and loved, for more than thirty years. From the Broads at the top to the Lower Woodford hatches at the bottom, scarcely a bend or pool fails to evoke memories. I suppose there were days when the river was dour, but looking back it is all bathed in a golden glow of friends and laughter and memorable fish.

One of the attractions of the Heale water is that, thanks to Major Rasch's enlightened policy, it is lightly fished. I rate it highly. Unfortunately, there have been rather too many changes of keeper. If it had had a Lunn or a Sawyer, it would be even better.

Charles Jardine, a leading authority on casting and entomology, fishing at
Netton on the Avon. The bridge in the background was once the site
of a ford where, it is said, Charles II lost a horseshoe while
escaping from Oliver Cromwell.

After the Heale water the three miles (4.8 km) down to Stratford belong to the Salisbury Club which are very popular, especially at mayfly time.

Salisbury (pop. 40,000) is a historic city and was even, in mediaeval times, a port. Boats somehow made their way up the Avon and went down to the coast loaded with cloth or wool. Salisbury supplied a ship, called the *Trout*, for the Navy in the Hundred Years War with France. Nowadays it is a prosperous market city with a rich cultural life, stemming from its ecclesiastical heritage.

In the area of Salisbury, four tributaries enter the Avon. Two are comparatively long, and important from a fishing point of view – the Nadder and the Wylye. They will be dealt with separately. Two are minor – the Bourne and the Ebble, and they can be dealt with here.

The Bourne

The Bourne is another example of a fine little chalk stream which has fallen on evil days, due to water abstraction in the upper reaches. It used to run for 15 miles (24.1 km), from above Tidworth, due south to Salisbury, where it enters the Avon beside the 'B&Q' car park on the Southampton Road. Nowadays only the last 6 miles (9.6 km) below Porton are fishable. At the village of Newton Toney, 3 miles (4.8 km) above Porton, the river has only run, in the last few years, for a few weeks after the floods of January 1990. Otherwise, there is a bed of rough grass and rank weeds, where once was a sparkling stream.

Below Porton, at East Gomeldon, there is a mile (1.6 km) of good fishing in private hands, where the water level is kept up by one of the few hatches still in working order, and in May the banks are profuse with orchids. At Hurdcott, the Salisbury Club have a short, but pretty stretch. Since the demise of the old Figsbury Fishing Club some 25 years ago, that is all, as far as serious fishing is concerned.

Where the Bourne reaches the Southampton Road, and the Salisbury Club had its beginnings in 1941, a planning blunder has allowed a new industrial estate to encroach up to the bank. It should have been kept at least 30 ft (9.1 m) back.

Pike seem to like the Bourne, as do grayling, and some salmon still run up to spawn. But its glory as a fishery has largely gone. It is a pity that the Salmon and Trout Association, who are supposed to fight abstractions, are such a toothless organisation, without the financial resources to fight these cases through the courts.

The Wiltshire Bourne, an example of the smallest kind of chalk stream which can nevertheless hold large fish.

The Ebble

The Ebble has been fortunate. It is still an outstanding little stream, running for about 7 miles (11.2 km) from west to east and joining the Avon at Bodenham, about 1½ miles (2.4 km) below Salisbury. It is only about 15–20 ft (4.5–6 m) wide. It is all privately owned, mostly by local farmers, though Lord Head and Lord Radnor each have short stretches. It is non-commercial, with the owners looking after their own stretches, and one or two small syndicates.

A most welcome feature is that it is not stocked. It produces fine healthy wild fish averaging 1½ lb (.68 kg), with some of 2 lb (.9 kg) and the odd specimen of 3 lb (1.36 kg). Nor does it suffer from pollution. There are no fish farms. The land either side is grazed, not ploughed. It has suffered from abstraction and drought, but nothing like so severely as the Bourne.

The old Wessex Water Authority did wanton damage to part of the Ebble in the early eighties, by widening and deepening the stream in the name of land drainage. Over the centuries, chalk streams form a bed of gravel mixed with chalk. It is impervious, and quite thin, and to remove it by dredging is asking for trouble. The bed silts up and the current becomes sluggish. Ranunculus will not grow. Mr Simon Cain, the fisheries consultant, whose work on the Wylye is described on page 112, has done much to restore the river by narrowing it to increase the flow and planting ranunculus.

Salisbury to the Sea

Below Salisbury the Avon changes its character. It receives the waters of the Nadder, Wylye, Bourne and Ebble. It divides into several channels – known locally as 'braiding' – a legacy of old irrigation systems. The countryside consists of flat meadows, the gradient of the river is slight, the flow is slow, and coarse fish predominate.

But to dismiss the middle and lower Avon for this would be quite wrong. It has been a Mecca for coarse fishers from all over the United Kingdom, many of whom dream of one day catching

THE WYLYE, NADDER AND EBBLE

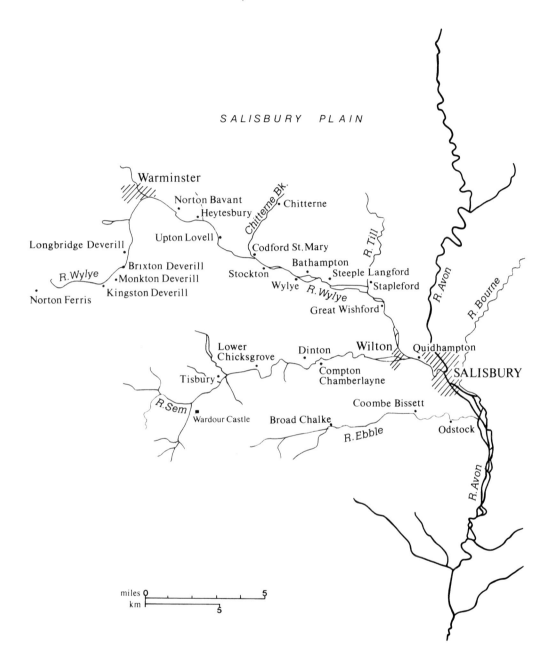

SALISBURY PLAIN

Warminster

Norton Bavant

Heytesbury

Chitterne Bk.

Chitterne

R. Till

Longbridge Deverill

Upton Lovell

Codford St. Mary

Bathampton

R. Wylye

Brixton Deverill

Stockton

Steeple Langford

R. Avon

Monkton Deverill

Wylye

R. Wylye

Stapleford

Norton Ferris

Kingston Deverill

Great Wishford

R. Bourne

Lower
Chicksgrove

Dinton

Wilton

Quidhampton

Tisbury

Compton
Chamberlayne

SALISBURY

R. Sem

Wardour Castle

Broad Chalke

Coombe Bissett

R. Ebble

Odstock

R. Avon

miles 0   5
km   5

a 2-lb (.9 kg) roach. The Avon offered a chance of this. Inns and hotels along the river did a flourishing trade.

I believe that the skill of the top-class coarse fisher is probably greater than that of the fly fisher. He is dealing with a dozen or so different species, with different feeding habits. He practises catch and release and the fish become very wary. Of course, fly fishing is more active, and more exciting, but coarse fishing is more subtle, and more complex. I am not prepared to sit out all night under a green umbrella to catch a monster carp, like the late Richard Walker, but I admire those who do.

About 1975, a decline in the coarse fishing set in. The coarse fishers stopped coming, and there was a chorus of protest, led by that doughty campaigner and roach expert, Mr Gerry Swanton of Downton. What was the cause of the decline? The usual problems were cited – agricultural sprays, mechanical weed cutting which destroyed the eggs which adhered to the weeds, the decline of the water meadow system. But another factor was the large fish farm owned by Lord Radnor, about a mile upstream of Downton. It is said to be the largest in England, possibly in Europe. Many local anglers blamed pollution by the effluent from the fish farm for the Avon's troubles. It is on record that in the eighties, the fish farm regularly exceeded its discharge consents. It is also on record that the old Wessex Water Authority never brought a prosecution.

The Anglers Co-operative Association wished to do so but were prevented because they have no legal right to enter the fish farm to take water samples.

Thus, while it was never proved that the fish farm was the cause of the troubles, there was enormous public pressure on Lord Radnor to clean up the effluent, and in the last few years he has made great efforts to do so. The result has been that the fishing has markedly improved. Other fish farms lower down the river still present a problem, but now that the old Water Authority has been replaced by the National Rivers Authority, there is the prospect of much tougher and more decisive action. I am optimistic that the next few years will see an improvement.

Fordingbridge (pop 5,000) is a pleasant little New Forest town, frequented by bird watchers searching in the nearby Forest for the elusive Dartford Warbler. It has a venerable stone bridge of seven arches over the Avon, and benefits from the construction of a by-pass some years ago.

About 5 miles (8 km) below Fordingbridge is the village of Ibsley, and from here to the sea, salmon fishing becomes predominant. The fisheries from Ibsley downstream are:

Somerley (3½ miles/5.6 km) owned by Lord Normanton
Several (2½ miles/4 km) owned by Mr R. Ferguson
Bisterne (5½ miles/8.8 km) owned by Major John Mills
Avon Tyrell (2 miles/3.2 km) owned by Lord Manners
Winkton (2 miles/3.2 km) owned by Major John Mills

And finally, at Christchurch, is the Royalty fishery of only three quarters of a mile, but the most productive of all, both for salmon and coarse fishing. The Royalty is owned by the West Hants Water Co, one of the 28 statutory water companies, many of which since privatisation have been taken over by French interests. West Hants are now owned by the Biwater Co Ltd. So far, this has not affected the fishing.

The Royalty attracts coarse anglers in large numbers. Barbel up to 14 lb (6.4 kg) are caught, as well as large roach and chub. Recently bream and carp have also appeared, which I am told indicates a decline in water quality. Salmon catches over the years have averaged about 150. In 1990, the total was 104, which considering the drought was still good. But it masked a decline in weight per fish, which was well down. The salmon season runs from 1 February to 30 September. The run of big spring fish has virtually ceased: most of the fish now are grilse.

As regards sea trout, it is no good mincing words: it has been a disaster. From ten years ago, when 1,500 was considered below average, they have declined to 50 in 1990. Col David Ransley, the Fishery Manager, says that plenty of sea trout could be seen in the well-known Bridge Pool at Christchurch, but they did not run up the river. Because of low water? The netsmen at Mudeford have had an average year for sea trout, which indicates that the problem lies in the river itself rather than out at sea. Mr David Solomon, the fishery biologist, is carrying out investigative work into the problem.

Figures for the river as a whole are:

	Salmon		Sea Trout	
	Nets	**Rods**	**Nets**	**Rods**
1986	685	1047	317	2033
1987	568	601	378	1220
1988	556	708	467	698
1989	337	441	333	341
1990	266	295	461	57

THE NADDER

The Nadder is the odd stream out. It is not a true chalk stream although it runs close to the Wylye, which is. It rises in the Donheads and is joined by the Sem Brook, both lying in the greensands which stretch half way down its 22 miles (35.4 km). The river bed is clay, with steep banks which make wading usually necessary. It is subject to spates, rising quickly after heavy rain and taking two or three days to clear. Ranunculus is less plentiful and therefore fly-life is sparse, though the mayfly is good most years. Where there is a gravel bed, it is dark and of poor quality, but trout do spawn naturally. They grow slowly, but live long – up to eight years, much longer than farm-reared fish. With these drawbacks, is the Nadder a poor fishing river? Far from it, as we shall see.

In the fairly acid water, coarse fish thrive, and the first fishery from the source, the Tisbury Angling Club, are coarse fishers. They co-operate happily with the next fishery downstream, the Teffont Fishing Club, which has 4 miles (6.4 km) of water from Lower Chicksgrove down to half a mile (.8 km), above Dinton Mill. The club had its origins in 1913 and is remarkable for the number of long serving officers and members. Colonel Kennedy Shaw, the founder, served the club as secretary and chairman for 47 years. Moody, the first keeper, who was said to have spent so much time hunting pike that he had grown to look like one, served for 14 years. Wilkins, the next, did 36 years. Major General David Price, the present chairman, has so far reached 21 years.

Such long service shows the affection that the Nadder inspires, and walking the banks, it is easy to see why. The Nadder valley is beautiful. As General Price writes in the club history: 'In spite of the occasional Waterloo to Exeter train, the Nadder valley is a peaceful place where the fisherman can be happy.' The railway and the river are intertwined here, but the noise of one or two trains an hour is friendly and quite acceptable, unlike the constant roar of traffic which spoils some parts of the Wylye.

The Teffont Club has 34 members, who describe themselves as 'a band of friends rather than a highly organised club'. They stock every year with yearlings which grow on, albeit slowly, and supplement the wild fish. The average size caught is about 12 ozs (.34 kg). In one stretch they have introduced a few rainbows, of no great size. It is to the credit of the members that they do not demand the stocking of over-size monsters from fish farms. Up to a few years ago, they had a full-time keeper and their own hatchery, where they would breed from the native stock. Hard economics and inflation have forced the abandonment of the hatchery and there is now only a part-time keeper. But the club flourishes. A proposal a few years ago to supplement the income with day tickets was greeted with horror by the majority. They take some 300 to 400 fish per season, the majority by the end of

Ed Zern, the great American humorous writer, fishing on the Avon.

the mayfly. After that the river is quiescent until September, when fly-life reappears. The Teffont Club is a model. Long may it continue. The next fishery could not provide a greater contrast.

This is the Compton Chamberlayne fishery of some 2½ miles (4.0 km), owned by Mr Newman. It is centred on Dinton Mill, where the keeper, Mr Charles Patrick, has a cottage and stew ponds. The old millhouse has been modernised and furnished to a standard which can justifiably be called luxurious. It is now let on the Time Share system, and is, to the best of my knowledge, the only example of this on the chalk streams, though of course, it is common on the Scottish salmon rivers. The fishery is divided into seven beats. One is kept for the Time Share occupant, one for day tickets, and five for a syndicate of full, half, or quarter rods. During the season, they stock with two thirds browns and one third rainbows up to 3 lb (1.36 kg), with some bigger. Stocking takes place every fortnight. It is, to speak plainly, a put-and-take fishery. It is a commercial operation, and a very successful one. All the Time Share vacancies were snapped up when Savills put them on the market a few years ago. But it puts heavy pressure on the river, which is, in my view, undesirable.

Burcombe Club

Below Compton Chamberlayne, we return – thankfully – to a fishery run by a happy group of friends – the Burcombe Club. Their water starts at Barford St Martin and goes down to Wilton, about 2 miles (3.2 km) in all. At Burcombe Bridge, half way down the water, the Nadder begins to change, and to become a typical chalk stream. The greensand is finished and the river, as it flows through the chalk, receives pure alkaline water from many springs.

They stock with browns and a few rainbows up to 1½ lb (.68 kg) and have at present 23 members. Pike have been largely eliminated by electric fishing, but carp are a problem. Some years ago, there was an escape of carp from an ornamental pond, and they have become a pest. In 1990, 130 were taken out by electric fishing, including one of 15 lb (6.8 kg). Carp spawn in May and the recent warm weather in May will have helped them to thrive.

They are herbivores, unlike trout which are carnivores, but they eat weed and thus are undesirable in a chalk stream.

Fifty years ago, Mr Bruce Turner (now 80) told me all the fish were wild. Now they have to rely on stocking, and the fly life – apart from the mayfly – is not what it might be. But still the members stay loyal. 'I have always loved the Nadder valley,' said Mr Turner. 'Mind you, nowadays some of us don't do much fishing. We just sit on a bench and talk.' Well, that too has its place. It is not all of fishing to fish.

Wilton and Wilton House

Although the little town of Wilton was the ancient capital of Wessex and gave its name to the county of Wiltshire – and is far older than the present city of Salisbury – it is today a pleasant but unremarkable place. It lives under the beneficent shadow of the Herbert family, the Earls of Pembroke, whose stately home, Wilton House attracts 100,000 visitors a year. There is a legend that Shakespeare himself, with his troupe of players, gave the first performance of *Twelfth Night* at the house. Wilton House is a treasure house of Old Masters, including Rembrandt, Tintoretto, and Van Dyck in the magnificent Double Cube room. No visitor to the chalk streams should miss it.

The present Earl fishes in the grounds of the house, where he has about a mile (1.6 km) of the Nadder, and has been known to take salmon there. He also takes a keen interest in the well being of the chalk streams.

At Quidhampton, 350 yards (320 m) downstream of the wall of Wilton Park, the Nadder is joined by the Wylye, and the combined river, now known as the Nadder, flows on for 2½ miles (4.0 km) until it joins the Avon at Salisbury. Just below the junction with the Wylye, the Wylye Fly Fishers have a stretch, known as the Lower Water. It is a big river here for a chalk stream, in some places too wide to cast across, but a fine fishery well looked after by Mr David Nickol and his assistants. Unfortunately it suffers from poaching. Below this, the Salisbury AC have the water for 3 miles (4.8 km) into Salisbury, and operate it as a mixed fishery. Trout fishing operates until 16 June, when coarse fishing opens. It is not to be despised. Good fish are taken here every year, especially during the mayfly.

The Nadder has its drawbacks, as has been mentioned, but taken overall it is a lovely river. Many fishermen are happy to fish it for a lifetime.

THE WYLYE

As recently as 1986, John Ashley Cooper wrote that 'the Wylye is a perfect example of an unspoilt chalkstream, flowing through delightful Wiltshire villages and countryside: what more could a keen dry fly man want?' Today, only seven years later, it is hard to believe that so much damage could have been done. The villages and the countryside are still delightful, but the river has suffered grievously – so much that it is on the NRA's list of endangered rivers. A succession of dry winters and summers have been aggravated by abstraction and a plague of swans. These matters are discussed later, but first to describe the fisheries.

The Wylye rises in the Deverills, 5 miles (8.0 km) south of Warminster. It flows in a northerly direction to the town and then turns south east to flow 22 miles (35.4 km) past Wilton, to join the Nadder at Quidhampton. All of this is pure chalk. With the Nadder to the south, the two rivers make a large 'V', coming closer together until they eventually meet below Wilton.

The Wylye has a number of important fisheries, the first being the Longleat fishery of 2½ miles (4.0 km), followed by the Sutton Veney water which adjoins the recently constructed Warminster by-pass. Then comes the Norton Bavant fishery, followed by the Piscatorial Society's 5½ miles (8.8 km) from Heytesbury (once the home of Siegfried Sassoon) down to Stockton. These are all first class fisheries, well managed, notable for good fly life and prolific natural spawning. The Salisbury Angling Club have an attractive stretch of ¾ mile (1.2 km) at Stapleford. Mr Aiden Maitland Robinson is the new owner of the Bathampton stretch which used to belong to Lord Hugh Russell, and this is followed by Mr Bob Merrick's water at Ballington of 2½ miles (4.0 km), where Mr Simon Cain has been carrying out some interesting experiments in river management.

Over recent years, the fishery had been neglected. The river had spread out, flow was sluggish, fly life poor, and wild fish had disappeared. Obviously, narrowing the river to improve the flow was required, and was put in hand. But Mr Cain's original contribution was this: when he narrowed the river, by driving in piles and laying horizontal logs, instead of the usual infilling with chalk and soil, he first laid down some 2 ft (.6 m) of heavy scrub, which would create an underwater cavern to encourage all kinds of invertebrates, including crayfish, and provide a refuge for fish. There has been extensive planting of ranunculus, which has thrived in the improved flow. Silt has been raked out, and wild fish have reappeared. Mayfly has been absent, but this has been more than made up by tremendous hatches of ephemoptera. The experiment has been a spectacular success.

Below Ballington is the well-known Wylye Fly Fishers Club, with about 50 members, and 2½ miles (4.0 km) down to Little Wishford. They stock three times a year with browns of about 1 lb (.45 kg) to supplement the wild fish. They make a condition that members must live at least 12 miles (19.5 km) away from the Wylye, and have a long waiting list. Next is the Wilton Fishing Club with 6 miles (9.6 km) down to Lord Pembroke's water in Wilton Park. They are the oldest of the clubs, going back to 1901. They now have 45 members, one of whom, a member of many years standing, told me that they have three kinds of member. 'First, there is the man who catches a lot of fish and is quite happy. Then there is the man who catches few fish, but is also happy. Finally, there is the man who catches few fish and is not happy. He departs after a season or two to seek pastures new and easier fishing.' The wild fish which still predominate offer a real challenge and attract the discerning fisherman, as is shown by the waiting list. Long may it continue.

That is a description of the fisheries. Now for the problems of the Wylye, which are twofold – abstraction and swans. There has been for some years a water abstraction point in the Deverills, but the quantities taken are small, and there is a compensation scheme to feed in water when the flow falls to a permitted minimum. It does little harm except when exacerbated by drought. The real damage is being done at Codford St Mary and Chitterne, about one third down the river.

In 1967 and 1973, when it was thought that there was an unlimited amount of water available in the underground aquifers, licences were granted for 6.1 million gallons of water a day to be taken from boreholes at Codford and Chitterne. This water is taken to towns to the north and west, out of the Wylye catchment area. In July 1990, when the long drought also began to have an effect, one riparian owner at Steeple Langford said: 'the river flow has collapsed.' The Chitterne Brook, a valuable spawning stream with some of the purest water, dried up completely and remained dry until early spring 1991. Perch appeared, and chub. Blanket weed made its noxious presence felt and ranunculus diminished. Only where work had been done to narrow the river, as at Ballington, and thus maintained a good current, did any semblance of a healthy chalk stream remain.

What little ranunculus survived the floods of January 1990, which ripped out the roots, was grazed off by swans which infest

A lady fly fisher on the Wylye.

the Wylye in very large numbers. They go up the river eating ranunculus like a Hoover. Frank Sawyer called them supercilious. I find their beauty coldly repellent. One day fishing the Wylye, I had the feeling I was being overlooked. Turning around, I saw about twenty swans at about the length of my back cast, obviously wanting me to move on so that they could get at the weed. It was unnerving.

Some of the fisheries have been planting water milfoil, an excellent weed for the chalk streams, which has the advantage that it comes into flower in July after the ranunculus and swans do not like it. But it is expensive in time and labour.

It would be the easiest thing in the world to control the swans' numbers. They need not be shot. They could be captured and taken to places where they are welcome, such as the coarse fishing rivers where they have been killed, by eating angler's lead shot.

Their eggs could be pricked. But none of these things can be done without special permission, for swans are protected. And the permission has not been forthcoming. The Ministry of Agriculture exists to foster farming, not fishing. If the swans were damaging crops, they would be interested. When the swans eat river weed, they are not concerned. There is powerful opposition from the RSPB and the Nature Conservancy Council. The situation is absurd. Culling of a species has to be done from time to time to preserve a balance. Conservation has degenerated into sentimentality.

If the swan problem is a matter of political will, and could be solved with little expense – as, surely, it will be – abstraction is another thing. People must have water. There are more and more of them, for they like to live among the chalk streams – and who can blame them? But if the Wylye is to be saved, the abstraction licenses must be revoked. This will mean that the Water Supply plc must obtain its water elsewhere: either by pumping it back from the mouth of the river, or by constructing new reservoirs which would be filled from the winter rains. These measures are expensive. The Water Supply plc would have to be compensated for the loss of their abstraction license. No one that I have spoken to is prepared to put a figure on it, except to say that it will be some millions of pounds.

The Wylye is on the NRA's list of endangered rivers, and a full-scale scientific investigation into the state of the river has begun. But it will not be completed until 1994. Until then, the outlook for the Wylye is grim – unless, of course, the recent trend is reversed and we get a succession of wet winters. And that is in the lap of the gods.

THE FROME AND PIDDLE

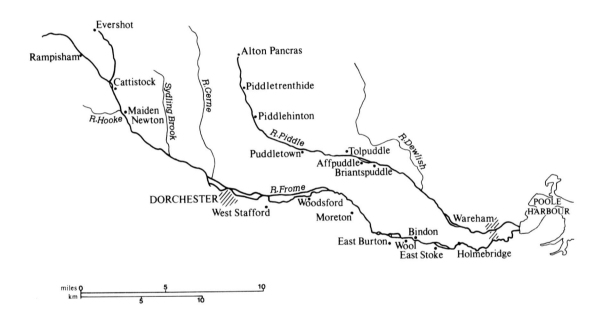

4

THE RIVERS OF
DORSET

Frome

Allen

Piddle

—— A FEW WORDS ABOUT DORSET ——

Among its many virtues, it contains some of the very best of the chalk streams: from the Frome, the biggest, to the smaller Allen and Piddle, to tiny streams like the Cerne, the Sydling, or the Shreen. In width they may be little more than ditches, yet they wind about through the Dorset valleys full of wild and lusty trout. Fortunate is the man who lives by the Cerne!

———— THE FROME ————

The Dorset Frome, which rises near Evershot in west Dorset, runs eastward for 35 miles (56.3 km) before it reaches the sea in Poole Harbour, a mile or so below the town of Wareham. It should not be confused with the Somerset Frome which runs from the town of that name northwards to join the Bristol Avon.

It is in every sense a major chalk stream, to be ranked with the best. Indeed, in the summer of 1991 it was in better condition than most. It has plentiful weed growth, good flow, and clear water. The level may be down, but not disastrously. Here is a rarity – a chalk stream not suffering from pollution or abstraction.

For some reason, or pure chance, there is no literary heritage on the Frome. Roderick Haig Brown, author of *A River Never Sleeps*, was a Dorset man, but he went to North America and wrote about the rivers there. I have found only the briefest references to the Frome in his writings. What little is known outside Dorset derives from Aylmer Tryon's articles about the salmon fishing on the lower reaches, and John Ashley Cooper's 1986 book *A Ring of Wessex Waters*.

The first 14 miles (22.5 km) of the Frome, from the source to Dorchester, provides chalk stream fishing of a high class, and if it was developed, with a higher standard of keepering, it could be even better. The country could hardly be lovelier, with the river winding through meadows, with spinneys, old villages with churches of mellowed stone, and the gently curving slopes of the downs. From Rampisham down to Maiden Newton the river is in the hands of a number of private owners with no organised fishing. They may, and no doubt do, amuse themselves with the wild fish. In past years, there were organised syndicates.

The first organised and keepered fishery is that of Mr Richard Slocock, of the Wessex Fly Fishing School at Tolpuddle, who has ¾ mile (.2 km) at Maiden Newton. He takes his pupils there and keeps it stocked with browns.

At Cruxton, Mr Reg Smith has a syndicate fishing the 1½ miles (2.4 km) to the upper bridge at Frampton. From here down to the lower Frampton bridge, about ¾ mile (1.2 km), Dr Peck has a syndicate. Next, down to Gascoyne Bridge, is Mr Christopher Pope's water, about two miles (3.2 km), with two beats on the main river and one on the Sydling Brook. Mr Pope, of Wrackleford House, is connected with Eldridge Pope, the Dorchester brewers. A syndicate fishes his water, which is properly keepered. As far as is known, only browns are stocked in any of these fisheries and, indeed, some of them are still entirely wild. The river is much as all chalk streams were a century ago – charming, natural, a touch unkempt, and in the main, lightly fished.

We now come to the middle Frome and the Dorchester Fishing Club water of about 6 miles (9.6 km) – 3 miles (4.8 km) above the town and 3 miles below, and including side streams such as the Wrackle and the Stinsford carrier, along which Thomas Hardy walked to school by 'the embowered path beside the Frome'. The club was founded in 1877 by a Captain Dymond, who obtained a lease of the waters from the Duchy of Cornwall who are still the owners, and are the largest landowners in Dorchester. The Town Council's agreement was required and they exacted a price – six Town Rods were to be made available in perpetuity. There are now 55 rods, in addition to the Town Rods, who may fish for up to 50 days a season, which runs from 1 April to 14 October. Occasional Day Tickets are allowed outside the mayfly. There is a good head of wild fish, but after the mayfly they stock with browns of about 1¼ lb (.56 kg). About 700 fish are taken each season. There is a part-time keeper. This is an inexpensive, well-run club, and provides a fine amenity for local people.

The water is attractive, both above and below the town, with good hatches of fly, and is in better condition than more famous rivers to the east. The grayling population is on the increase, which is a good sign of water purity. Louds Mill, below the town, is a favourite spawning area for salmon, and they were seen there in large numbers in the winter of 1990–91 – another good sign.

The Dorchester Fishing Club water extends down to Lower Bockhampton bridge, and from here we find the river divided into carriers by the old irrigation system. A decision was taken a few years ago to remove all the hatches, and it is interesting to see the difference from a river such as the Kennet, where they have been retained.

The river flows freely, there is a complete absence of silt and mud, the bed is of good clean gravel, but in a time when we are still suffering from the effects of three dry winters, levels are very low, and some carriers are practically dry. It is the lesser of two evils.

The next fishery is that of Mr R. Belgrave – a short stretch stocked with browns, fished by the owner and friends – and then another short stretch rented by Mr R. Pavitt of Stafford House. Mr Pavitt has four self-catering flats which he lets with the fishing. He has about ⅓ mile of the river and part of the South Winterbourne, a tributary which joins the Frome at West Stafford.

Brigadier S. N. Floyer Acland then has about ¾ mile (1.2 km), part on the river and part on a carrier known as the North Stream. One could not wish for prettier water, but for some mysterious reason most of the wild fish have disappeared. Only a few large grayling are visible. There is an unwelcome weed called water dropwort and some Canadian pondweed: whether this is the cause is not known.

Hardy called this area The Vale of the Great Dairies. Lower Lewell Farm was 'Talbothays', where Tess, in *Tess of the d'Urbevilles*, was a milkmaid. There have been changes – the cattle are no longer red and dun, but black and white, and the 'drowns' where Tess and Angel Clare walked have fallen into disuse. But it is still lush, fertile, farming country.

Below this, apart from some small stretches, the Ilsington Estate have about two miles (3.2 km), and Mr W. Paul of Woodsford Farms has a stretch of 1½ miles (2.4 km). All this water is obviously unfished: it is neglected, with unkempt banks and thick masses of weed from bank to bank. Why, one wonders? If this was Hampshire, the weed would have been cleared, stocked browns or rainbows put in, and expensive rods let. But in Dorset, the pace of life beats slower.

At Pallington, where three lakes fed from the Frome are open for coarse and rainbow trout fishing, the lake owner also has half a mile (.8 km) of the river which he retains for his own use, mainly for salmon. Then comes the salmon fishery belonging to Mrs Mary Frampton of Moreton, who has 1½ miles (2.4 km) of water either side of the village – 3 miles (4.8 km) in all, including a carrier. Some sixteen rods fish it, on a named day a week basis. It appeared to be in a healthy state, but Mrs Frampton tells me that the fishing in 1991 has not been good. A malaise has struck this part of the Frome, made more mysterious by the fact that some grayling are present, and salmon parr can be seen. A scientific investigation of the river is needed.

From Mrs Frampton's water at Moreton down to Wareham, a distance of 14 miles (22.5 km), the Frome is a salmon fishery. First is the East Burton water, belonging to the Digby Estate. The Army at Bovington Camp (depot of the Royal Armoured Corps) have a small stretch here – as they usually do when they are stationed by a river! Next is the Woolbridge Manor water of 1½ miles (2.4 km) on one bank, leased by Mr Maddox. In passing, this house was where Tess and Angel Clare spent their disastrous wedding night, in *Tess of the d'Urbervilles*.

Then follows the Bindon Abbey water of about two miles, belonging to the Weld Estate, which has been leased for nearly forty years to the Hon. Aylmer Tryon – who once, in the '60s, caught five salmon on a fly before breakfast – but the great majority of salmon are taken on bait, often a prawn fished 'sink and draw'. On a wet and windy day in March of 1991, when well into his ninth decade, Aylmer Tryon caught an 18-lb (8.17 kg) fish and landed it without assistance.

Below Bindon is the Institute of Terrestrial Ecology water of about three miles (4.8 km), at East Stoke, fished by seven rods who took 30 fish in 1990. The Institute has an electronic fish counter on the river and their figures for salmon ascending the Frome are as follows:

1986	2795
1987	3415
1988	4183
1989	3200
1990	2357

The conclusion is that in the drought years of '89 and '90, the salmon run on the Frome has held up better than on the Itchen, Test, or Avon. Rods normally catch about 10 per cent of the total run – a low percentage which is caused by the fact that there are peculiar difficulties to the Frome. It is small, compared to the Avon, and the banks are high. Fish tend to hug the banks and are easily scared. So the cast must be accurate and the angler must keep well back, not an easy formula.

The Institute does much valuable research into the rivers and as their Government funding has been reduced, they are keenly looking for projects and backing from bodies such as the NRA or local authorities.

After this, from Holme Bridge down to the Wareham bridge there are the Longmead water, the Joint Water, the Priory water, the Encombe Estate water, and a stretch belonging to Cdr. Walter Drax. In all, ten rods fish these waters. Below Wareham, the last 2 miles (3.2 km) of tidal waters is owned by the NRA and it is said to be a good coarse fishery for roach and dace.

One feature of the river from Bindon down must be remarked upon. The countryside is flat and marshy, rather like the Avon below Ringwood, but the river twists like a writhing snake, often turning a full 180 degrees in convolutions and serpentine twists.

Sea trout are also taken on the Frome up as far as Bindon, but not in any great numbers (38 in 1989 and 29 in 1990). However, those that are taken are often large. A net operates in Poole Harbour but the numbers of fish it takes are not great – in 1990, 78 salmon and 32 sea trout some of which would have run up the Piddle.

THE ALLEN

The Allen is a lovely little stream, reminiscent of the Ebble. Its course runs through some of the finest countryside in all Dorset. The chalk downs are soft and gentle, unlike the steep downs of the upper Avon. They please the eye, but they have a disadvantage, for these downs are like giant sponges, holding water to feed the rivers. The lower the downs, the less water they hold. Thus, nature has made the Allen susceptible to drought, and man has compounded it. A tragedy hangs over this jewel of a river.

The troubles of the Allen stem from the permission granted many years ago to the Bournemouth Water Co, to abstract up to 5 million gallons a day from a borehole situated close to the river at Stanbridge Mill, about two thirds of the way down its 13-mile (20.9 km) course. In summer, the whole flow of the river is not much more than this, so it is not surprising that the result has been disastrous. A compensation scheme is in operation, to pump water from the chalk aquifer some 2 miles (3.2 km) above the source. Without this, the Allen would have died: but is an alleviation, not a solution. The NRA have commissioned a study into the Allen, as an endangered river, and it may be that the license to abstract will be revoked. In that case, the water company will have to be compensated and that will be expensive. The cost, of course, will fall on the taxpayers. Who else?

In the winter of 1990-91 the Winterbourne above the village of Monkton Up Wimborne failed to run at all. Downstream from

Sidney Vines fishing the Allen below Stanbridge Hill. The Allen has suffered from abstraction.

Monkton, where the river begins, it was still flowing well, with good ranunculus, and appeared healthy – but one dreads to think what will happen in another dry summer.

The first fishery, at the village of Wimborne St Giles, is the 4½ miles (7.24 km) owned by the Shaftesbury estate. On the edge of the village is St Giles House, a stately home and formerly the home of the Earl of Shaftesbury. It is no longer lived in, but the estate offices are there.

The Shaftesbury family (family name Ashley Cooper) have been at St Giles since the fifteenth century. The seventh Earl was the humanitarian and social reformer who succeeded in 1847 in passing laws through Parliament to end the worst abuses of the Industrial Revolution, such as child labour.

The estate water is organised in an unusual way. Tickets are sold for either two days (Wednesday and Thursday) or three days

THE ALLEN

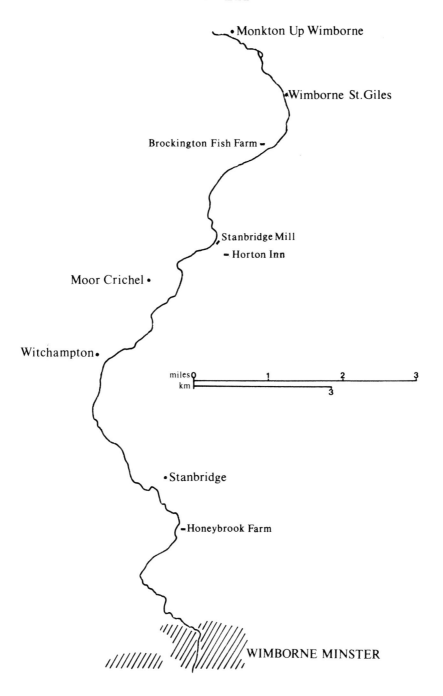

- Monkton Up Wimborne

- Wimborne St. Giles

Brockington Fish Farm —

Stanbridge Mill
— Horton Inn

Moor Crichel •

Witchampton •

miles 0   1   2   3
km

• Stanbridge

— Honeybrook Farm

WIMBORNE MINSTER

(Friday, Saturday, Sunday). On Monday and Tuesday the water is rested – as it should be. There are too many seven-day-a-week fisheries. Stocking is done at the beginning of the season with 300 browns of 12–14 in. (30.4–35.5 cm), which come from the estate's own fish farm at Brockington, a mile (1.6 km) below Wimborne St Giles, which does not appear to harm the river.

Only three rods are allowed per day and it is very popular, being booked up from year to year. I have met an American fisherman who has come over every year for 19 years to stay at the Horton Inn and fish the Allen. He is a good judge of a chalk stream. This seems to me yet another example of the fact that the further you go from London, and the glamour of the Hampshire rivers, the better value the fishing.

Below the Shaftesbury water there are two stretches, at Crichel (1½ miles/2.4 km) and from Witchampton to Honeybrook (3 miles/4.8 km) operated by private syndicates. Below this is ¾ mile (1.2 km) owned by the National Trust – it is part of the Kingston Lacey estate which the last member of the Bankes family willed to the National Trust a few years ago. This is leased to Mr John Bass. Finally, the Wimborne Angling Club have half a mile (.8 km) of mixed coarse and game fishing until the Allen joins the Stour (which is not a chalk stream) at Wimborne Minster, which is notable for its great twin-towered church, parts of which date back to Norman times. Wimborne is still a most attractive old Dorset market town.

The Allen Association, led by Col. Bill Humphries and Mr Harry Teasdale has fought hard for the Allen. The arrival of the NRA gives ground for guarded optimism. But the main battle over abstraction has still to be won.

THE PIDDLE

The Piddle, or what remains of it after abstraction, is another enchanting Dorset stream. For, as so often in these pages, we find a river shorn of its full length, retaining enough of its former glory to let us see what it was once like over the whole of its 22 miles (35.4 km).

It is one of the narrowest of the chalk streams, averaging about 15 feet (4.5 m) across except in the pools. Down to Afpuddle it is pure chalk, but below that the soil is clay and the scenery beomes heathland with conifers, rather like the New Forest. Through it runs the charming little Piddle, quite remote from the works of man. In places it is approached by tracks through woods – not metalled roads – and you will find no motor cars, no trains, no aeroplanes, nothing at all but serenity and beauty and balm for the spirit. And good fishing to boot!

The Piddle rises at Alton Pancras, 8 miles (12.8 km) north of Dorchester. After six miles (9.6 km) it reaches Puddletown, after which it turns east and flows on for 16 miles (25.7 km) to Poole Harbour, where it emerges about half a mile (.8 km) to the north of the Frome. The town of Wareham lies between the two rivers. Nowadays, the Piddle is dry from June onwards above Puddletown. The reason is the usual one – abstraction – caused by the insatiable demand of the vast urban sprawl of Bournemouth for water. One million gallons a day are taken from the source at Alton Pancras, six million from Briantspuddle and three million from the Devils Brook at Dewlish. Of course, a small river like the Piddle cannot sustain this. It is no wonder that the effects have been so dire.

Our description of the fishing must therefore begin at Puddletown, omitting the top 6 miles (9.6 km), now dry, where once a lovely stream flowed through Dorset villages like Piddle-trenthide and Piddlehinton, and provided fine fishing.

Puddletown is a large village, called by Thomas Hardy 'Weatherbury'. It is notable for the village church which escaped the attentions of Victorian restorers and still has its musicians' gallery at the west end, where the old village 'quire' sang, before the new-fangled organ appeared – and where the modern 'choir' still sings. It is a fine old church, and in *Far From the Madding Crowd* Fanny Robin was buried in the churchyard and Sergeant Troy put flowers on her grave. He slept in the porch, while the rain poured down, and woke in a gloomy dawn to see water spouting from a gargoyle on to the grave and washing his flowers away – a typical Hardy scene of an unkind fate.

The first fishery below Puddletown is that of Mr H. Wood Homer of Bardolf Manor. There are still good fly hatches here, and natural spawning, producing fish of about 1 lb (.45 kg) with an occasional fish of over 3 lb (1.36 kg). We then come to the village of Tolpuddle, famous for its martyrs.

At Tolpuddle, Mr Richard Slocock runs the Wessex Fly Fishing School with organised courses on one mile of the Piddle and a lake. The river is stocked with browns and the lake with rainbows. The river here is small and winding through open meadows, while the lake is pleasant. It fulfils its purpose of teaching fly fishing admirably. Several small fisheries in private hands follow, including a short stretch at Chamberlayn's Farm belonging to the Army from the nearby Bovington Camp. At Hyde, there used to be a fine fishery, but the house is now a country club and the present owners appear not to be interested in the fishery.

Below Hyde is the Trigon Estate of Mr Giles Sturdy, with 1½ miles (2.4 km) of the most charming water. It is quite idyllic – here one is in the depths of deepest Dorset, far from the madding crowd, and in particular from the noise of the madding motor car. It is not typical chalk stream scenery, more like the New Forest with firs and heath. It has unusual features. Mr Sturdy's grandfather, Mr Leonard Sturdy, was a Victorian engineer as well as a riparian owner, and a keen fisherman. When he built weirs, he made them architectural features. He also built lovely small stone bridges. Fishing here, you can see hobbies taking mayflies, kingfishers, grey wagtails, and pick (in season) wild strawberries. Miss Phillida Sturdy – Mr Giles Sturdy's sister – who looks after the fishery and the forestry, told me a tale of her grandmother. She endured endless talk at the table of a very large trout which no one could catch. Declaring she would have no more of it, she took a rod, baited the hook with bread paste, and caught the fish – to the fury and consternation of her husband.

Mr Leonard Sturdy was mainly interested not in the trout, but in the salmon. Up to 1986 salmon were regularly caught at Trigon, including one of 34½ lb (15.6 kg), by Mr T. Ingram, in 1985. But no more are caught today, though plenty are seen running up to spawn in October and November, when the season is over. So one day, salmon may be caught again at Trigon. The estate has its own fish farm on the river, which seems not to harm it, and provides rainbows for the fishery. The estate lets one-day-a-week season rods, two fishing during the day and two in the evenings. The pressure is thus quite heavy, which is a pity, as is the stocking with rainbows.

Below, the NRA owns about 1½ miles (2.4 km) of tidal water below Wareham, which they let out to season rods for salmon and sea trout. In 1989, the Piddle recorded 19 salmon and 11 sea trout. In 1990, the figures were 13 and 8. A net operates in Poole Harbour, which takes fish which would have ascended the Frome or the Piddle, but the numbers are not great.

The main hope for the Piddle is the NRA investigation (it has been classified as a 'sick' river) which reported in April 1991. There are a number of recommendations including one to revoke the abstraction licence, at Alton Pancras. This will involve compensation payable to the water company. Whether the political will exists to find the money – one figure quoted is 'at least £2 million' – remains to be seen. Those who love this river – and they are many – devoutly hope so.

THE KENNET
(chalk stream section only)

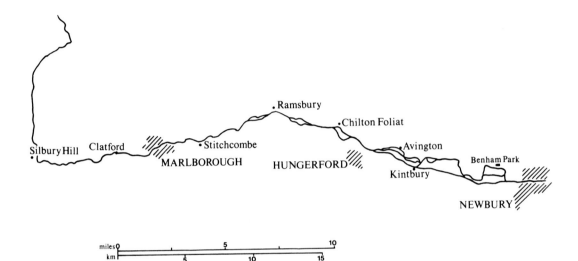

Note: Kennet and Avon Canal (not shown) runs parallel
to the river from Hungerford to Newbury.

5

THE RIVERS OF
BERKSHIRE

Kennet

Lambourn

Pang

Loddon

THE KENNET

The fishermen of the Kennet say that in its heyday it was superior to the Test. One might reply: 'They would say that, wouldn't they?' I doubt that any river was superior to the Test in *its* heyday: but today, when both rivers have declined, I think that the Kennet has declined less. It does not suffer from a proliferation of fish farms, or from agricultural pollution, and while some of it is over-fished, it has not degenerated into a put and take fishery as has so much of the Test. And while the Test has always been famous for the mayfly, the Kennet below Kintbury is phenomenal – the hatches have to be seen to be believed.

The Kennet's problem is simply stated – lack of water, caused by abstraction and drought. It is a chalk stream from its source, about 6 miles (9.6 km) west of Marlborough. There used also to be a winterbourne running north for another six or seven miles (9.6–11.2 km). This is now nearly all dry. The river begins to flow at Clatford, about two miles (3.2 km) west of Marlborough. The abstractions which have caused the damage are at Axford (9.3 million litres a day), Ogbourne St George (8.1 million litres per day), both of which supply water to the increasing population of Swindon, and Wansdyke and Cherhill which supply 5.4 million litres per day to Devizes and Calne. Abstraction is tolerable for a town along the river, like Marlborough, for 80 per cent is returned. But the water that goes to Swindon, Calne and Devizes is lost to the Kennet. A pressure group 'ARK' (Action for the River Kennet) has been formed to fight the abstractions and they are hopeful that new reservoirs will be constructed to supply Swindon. But this is long term. The NRA have commissioned a special study, but it is hard to see any rescue for the Kennet in the short term.

The Kennet continues a chalk stream as far as Newbury, where it becomes clay, and a coarse fishery, until it joins the Thames at Reading. Although it is only 22 miles (35.4 km) from Marlborough to Newbury, there are more than 80 miles (128.7 km) of fishable water.

This is because in addition to the natural turns and twists of the river, the old water engineers of the eighteenth century excelled themselves on the Kennet. They created a veritable maze of carriers, to irrigate the water meadows. In some places, four streams run abreast. In at least two, one stream is carried over another by an aqueduct. The water meadows are no longer irrigated – it is too labour intensive – but the valuable legacy of the carriers has been kept in good repair. It provides much needed variety, for some of the main river can be canal-like.

John Waller Hills knew the Kennet well, and said that its trout were the most difficult of all to land because they were so strong and made such intelligent use of weed. He was writing of the native Kennet trout, known as a 'greenback' (of which, sadly, few are left). The greenback was a silvery fish, without red spots, short, thick, with a large tail, and he fought like a tiger. Every year, a few greenbacks are caught. Attempts have been made to breed from them in hatcheries – so far without success. It will be a feather in the cap of the first keeper to succeed.

Dr J. C. Mottram (1880–1945) was another who knew the Kennet well, but he mentions it only briefly, as far as I can discover, in his writings. Mottram was an original fly designer, who was one of the first to design patterns to suggest the natural, rather than to try exact imitation. Modern writers, such as Arnold Gingrich, have done something to accord him the recognition he deserves. He wrote one outstanding book *Fly Fishing – Some New Arts and Mysteries* (1916). Mottram founded, in 1922, the Kennet Valley Fishery Association. This still flourishes. Practically all the riparian owners on the Kennet, Pang, and Lambourn are members. The present chairman is Mr Gerald Ward, CBE of Chilton Foliat, and his predecessor was Lord Rootes, who owns a short stretch of the Kennet opposite the Hungerford Town water.

The first fishery on the Kennet is in the grounds of Marlborough College on the south western edge of the town. The college owns about ¾ mile (1.2 km) and they are keen on their fishing. A master (known as a 'beak') is in charge and oversees a number of enthusiastic boys. Frank Sawyer used to take courses here in the Summer School, in the seventies, and they have named Sawyers Pool after him. The river is low and short of ranunculus, but there are still plenty of wild fish, up to 3 lb (1.36 kg), with a few browns stocked. Grayling are also plentiful, and are excellent sport for the boys. The Kennet is a good grayling river – an indication of the quality of the water. As previously stated, pollution kills the grayling first, before the trout.

The first fishery below Marlborough is the Savernake Fly Fishers, a syndicate of 30 season rods, who lease 3¼ miles (5.2 km) from the Crown Estates down to Stitchcombe. They stock twice a season with browns up to 1½ lb (.68 kg). Below this is Major Fisher's 1½ miles (2.4 km) down to Axford Farm, fished in much the same way with 18 season rods, but with rather bigger fish – up to 2½ lb (4.0 kg) Both these are pleasant fisheries, suffering like all of them from lack of water and lack of weed, but well keepered by Mr John Hounslow.

Mr Harry Hyams, the property tycoon, of Ramsbury Manor, owns a mile (1.6 km) which he keeps in his own hands. Then come two short stretches at the village of Ramsbury, the first owned by Mr Rodney McMahon and the other by Mrs Ball. Another short stretch is owned by Mr Martyn Aybib, which he also keeps in his own hands. Mr Aybib achieved fame with his horse Snurge, which won the St Leger.

Below Knighton, we come to a major fishery – the Littlecote Estate fishery of Sir Seton Wills, a member of the well-known tobacco family. The main house was sold a few years ago to Mr Peter de Savary, who sponsored the British America Cup challenge, but Sir Seton retains the estate of 7,000 acres including the fishing of about 4 miles (6.43 km), including half a mile (.8 km) of a carrier and half a mile of the Aldbourne, a once splendid tributary which is now almost dry.

There are 22 members of the Littlecote Fishing Club, who are free to fish when they like and where they like – there are no beats. As usual with such a system, the rods tend to fish once or twice a week and the river is not overfished. There is one main stocking, in March, of browns which have been brought on in a hatch pool, and two 'top ups' in early June (browns) and late July (rainbows). The keeper, Mr Peter Woolnough, is trying to wean the rods away from rainbows, but he is finding it difficult. I saw one long stretch below the hatch pool with plentiful ranunculus and some fine trout lurking on the gravel – all a chalk stream should be. There are still wild fish to be caught, even a few greenbacks. It is no wonder this is a popular fishery with a long waiting list.

Next is the Chilton Foliat fishery of about three miles (4.8 km) including carriers, with 32 rods fishing either one or two days a week. The keeper, Mr Steve Jones, works closely with Peter Woolnough with much the same policy of one main stocking a year and a small amount of topping up. There are said to be plenty of wild fish. A tendency, which I do not much like, is to mow the bank back several yards – to manicure it. Of course, the purpose is to make casting easier: but isn't this part of the challenge?

Hungerford and the Town Water

The Hungerford Town Water was given to the people of the town by John O'Gaunt (1340–99) as a reward for helping his army in a battle in the Wars of the Roses. The town had to struggle over the next few centuries to hold on to their fishing (and common) and the matter was not finally settled until 1617, in the reign of James I. That king, who was short of money, sold the Manor (including the fishing) to the town, who were to appoint Trustees, and the inhabitants were to have free fishing for ever. That rule still applies to those who live in 96 houses in the town, who are known as commoners. At present about six of them avail themselves of this right.

The fishing totals about 4 miles (6.4 km), half on the Kennet and half on its little tributary, the Dun. Considering the prox-

imity of the Bath Road, the town, and the main railway line, it is pleasant water. My preference is for the Dun, which is in open country to the west of the town, but some memorable fish have been caught on the town water at the Wine Cellar (so called because it was the custom to put bottles of wine there to cool) and at Bracket Hatch. Rods are allotted in various ways – full rods, mid-week rods, weekend rods, named day rods, and 'special category' rods. It must complicate the Secretary Treasurer's job. He is Lt. Col. Don Macey RE, a former Constable, who has devoted himself to the river for many years.

One name which will always be associated with the fishery is the late Dr Cecil Terry, the inventor of the dry fly 'Terry's Terror' – still popular on the water – which he told Dermot Wilson was designed to resemble Piccadilly Circus. Terry used to invite Frank Sawyer up for a day during the mayfly, which Sawyer said was better on the Kennet than on any other river he knew. Howard Marshall would come over from his cottage on the Lambourn to fish with Terry, and he described Terry's capture of a 3 lb 7 oz (1.58 kg) trout at Denford Bridge as 'one of the most perfect bits of fishing I have ever seen'. The mayfly began to decline in the sixties and has now vanished. It has happened before, about 1910, but it returned in the twenties and, no doubt, will do so again.

In the summer of 1991, the river was bare of weed and low, but clear and fishing was in full swing. Stocking takes place once a fortnight with rainbows of 1½ lb (.68 kg) and browns of 2 lb (.9 kg). 'It is a put-and-take fishery now,' said Don Macey, with some regret. It is, indeed, a pity.

From Hungerford to Newbury

Below Hungerford we begin to find the mass of carriers which I referred to earlier. The first fishery, at Denford, is almost entirely on carriers. It has 2¼ miles (3.52 km), with only 100 yds (91.4 m) on the main river. It is varied, wild, and attractive, but is hard fished. There are five season rods each day with day tickets also on one day a week. Mr Frank Wilson, the owner of the fishery, told me that the stocking is entirely with rainbows. Why? 'To keep the price down.' They stock once a fortnight in May, and monthly thereafter. This is another put-and-take fishery. Some wild browns spawn here and there and several of 3 lb (1.36 kg) have been taken this year. At the bottom end there is good mayfly, and this is now the beginning of the famed Kennet mayfly which continues down to Newbury.

Lord Howard de Walden is the owner of the next fishery at Avington. He is associated with racing, and was three times Senior Steward of the Jockey Club. Eight season rods have some 4 miles (6.43 km) of fishing. It could be more, but at present 4 miles (6.43 km) of carriers are not maintained. It is stocked every three weeks with browns of 1¼ lb (.8 kg) plus 'a few big rainbows'. The Kennet is a big river here, too wide to cast across, flowing in a stately way through sweeping curves. The flow is sluggish because the hatches are kept closed to hold up the water level, but this results in a build-up of silt and is a cause of the disappearance of ranunculus. Hatches are a dangerous tool in river management. Closing them produces short-term benefits but long-term problems.

The bank is mown back several yards and kept short like a lawn. It is manicured, which is not to my taste. There must be many guests, for 2,000 fish are stocked, of which some 900 are caught. This stretch has good mayfly, usually starting in the late afternoon.

Below Lord Howard de Walden we come to the Barton Court fishery of 2½ miles (4 km), of which 2 miles (3.2 km) is on carriers and half mile (.8 km) on the main river. It is varied, rural, and attractive, with a maze of carriers – at one point, four streams run more or less parallel. Most days, eight rods fish it. One day a week is a full rod and one day a fortnight is a half rod. One Mondays, day tickets are allowed. They stock fortnightly with 90 per cent browns and 10 per cent rainbows – around 500 fish a month. It is thus hard fished.

Next is the celebrated Wilderness fishery, part of Sir Richard Sutton's Benham Park estate and managed by Mr David Hopson of Newbury. It begins at Kintbury and continues for two miles (3.2 km) downstream. Again, there is a maze of carriers giving in all about eight miles (12.8 km) of fishing. The old water engineers were at their most sophisticated here, with some streams led over others by aqueducts. The variety is fascinating with something of everything – tiny, intimate, streams and wide, open stretches through meadows. There are runs over gravel and deep pools. It is the prettiest fishery on the Kennet and one of the most secluded. The world – and the A4 Bath Road – are shut out.

Up to 1972 it was, in fact, a wilderness – unkeepered and unstocked. At that time, the estate decided, like so many, that the fishery must produce an income and it was organised into a syndicate of twenty rods with a full-time keeper. There are now 24 rods. They stock with browns only of about 2½ lb (1.1kg). Recently, the members decided to put in 100 large browns, up to 6 lb (2.7 kg), for the mayfly season. John Goddard took the underwater photographs here for his book, with Brian Clarke, *The Trout and the Fly* (1980).

John Goddard finds he is able to fish with a dry fly throughout the season – a high tribute to the fishery. He used to catch one wild fish to three stocked, but now finds the proportion one in five.

The members have agreed to practise catch and release on the carriers, but to kill all fish taken on the main river. I hope their example will be followed by others, for it will avoid the heavy and excessive stocking which goes on, to the detriment of the river.

On 8 June 1991, visiting the river with John Goddard and Roy Eaton, I saw a hatch of mayfly duns which exceeded anything I have seen in 30 years of the chalk streams. As you walked down the bank, you seemed to be pushing your way through them. They were coming off the river in countless thousands. John Goddard said that the previous week, there were even more – the whole river was carpeted with them. The old writers used to liken it to a snowstorm and indeed it was.

Apart from the mayfly time, the river here is lightly fished. The Wilderness is the outstanding fishery on the Kennet.

After Sir Peter Michael's syndicate on ¾ mile (1.2 km) of water at Benham Marsh Farm, we come to the final major fishery, at Benham Park, on Sir Richard Sutton's estate, and managed by Mr Michael Stratton of Turners Tackle shop in Reading. Season rods fish 3 miles (4.8 km) of water, most of it on carriers. The rods fish six days a week and the water is rested on

John Goddard, the leading entomologist, fishing the Wilderness water on the
Kennet. The mayfly hatches here are exceptional.

Thursdays – another example which others might follow. They
stock four times a year with browns only, of about 2 lb (.9 kg).
Twelve rods fish two days between Monday and Wednesday,
and twelve others one day between Friday and Sunday. There is
very good mayfly. The main river is pretty, but the carriers run
straight as arrows across the meadows. The water level is low and
there is little weed, except unwelcome ribbon weed. The Kennet
greenback survives here, and Mr Stratton and the keeper, Tony
Taylor, have tried to breed from them – a most estimable project.

Conclusion

The Kennet runs near to some of the most densely populated country in England. Newbury and Reading have boomed. London is within easy reach along the M4. Despite this, the villages like Ramsbury, Chilton Foliat, and Kintbury keep their rural charm. Always, one sees the Berkshire chalk downs, those marvellous reservoirs of pure water which feed the Kennet. It is pure still, as is shown by the plentiful supply of freshwater shrimp which keep the trout in good condition. Lack of water is the danger to the Kennet, not pollution.

THE LAMBOURN

As fishermen speak of Plunket Greene's Bourne, so they speak of Howard Marshall's Lambourn, if they are fortunate to have read his *Reflections on a River* (1967).

Howard Marshall was a household name in the thirties for his cricket commentaries on the wireless, when television was unheard of. The nation sat, tense, before their loudspeakers while that urbane, public-school voice intoned: 'Larwood runs up to bowl – over goes his arm.' But the fame conferred by the BBC is transient – as soon as the voice is no longer heard, or the face disappears from our screens, the owner of it disappears too, as ephemeral as a hatch of blue-winged olives.

Marshall was a first-class fisherman with a gift for description, humour, philosophy, and observation. Here is an example of his descriptive powers:

There is no more beautiful time of day than the last hour or so when the white owl comes ghosting from the spinney, and the swallows make their last scimitar glances at the river . . .

THE LAMBOURN

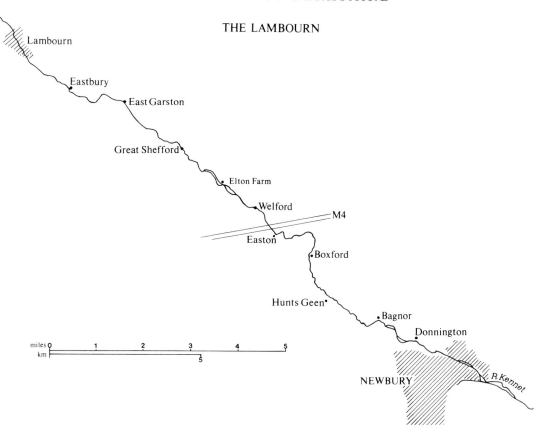

Here is some home-spun philosophy:

> There are, I think, two main classes of fly fishers – the Rushers
> and the Stickers. The Rushers are haunted by the belief that
> there is always a better fish rising round the next corner, so
> they are ever on the move rushing up the bank from rise to rise,
> confident that one day they will come upon Moby Dick. The
> Stickers are either more patient or more lethargic men, and
> having found what seems to them a promising place they stay
> there and wait for the trout to show themselves.

He advises us all, of course, to be Stickers.

The charm of the Lambourn – 'a small river running through a
gentle and exquisitely perfect valley' is what Marshall conveys.

Howard Marshall, whose name will always be associated with the river
Lambourn.

He ends:

> Simple things – so many of them – make up the angler's true
> delight. And all of them may be found on the banks of the little
> River Lambourn.

What of the Lambourn today? Marshall in 1967 was full of foreboding. He says that after a dry winter, the river was dry from the village of Lambourn down to Great Shefford. He thought this was exacerbated by abstraction at Lambourn. It still is practically dry (there is a trickle at Lambourn village in midsummer 1991) but there is no abstraction. The cause is three dry winters and changes in agriculture.

Below Great Shefford, there is enough water to make fishing possible and the Lambourn Fly Fishers, an informal club of thirty rods, have a mile (1.6 km). Their upper stretch is bare of cover and low in water, but their bottom water is better. Next comes a most delightful stretch at Elton Farm, managed by Mr Calkin of Boxford. It is tiny, intimate, winding, with good weed growth, pellucid water, and plenty of wild trout of a pound (.45 kg) or so. Marshall said that the Lambourn trout do not panic when they see you: they just sidle under the weeds. That is exactly what I found.

The stretch which follows is of about 2 miles (3.2 km) and is owned by Mrs Puxley of Welford Park. It is bisected by the M4 motorway, which Marshall thought would ruin the Lambourn.

It has not done that. The road is carried on pillars some 60 ft (18.2m) above the river. There is no run off of oil or tar from the road and the traffic cannot be seen – but of course it can be heard up to half a mile (.8 km) above and below the motorway. Unfortunately, this takes in Marshall's favourite Broadwater stretch, immediately above, and the river opposite, his cottage. The river is, however, still as he knew it. He could still fish and have fun.

Below Easton, the National Westminster Bank Fly Fishing Club have some water down to Boxford, where there is ¾ mile (1.2 km) fished by the Moor Bridge Farm syndicate of six rods. This again is lovely water, with good weed, fly life, and wild fish. Some browns are stocked, but it is questionable whether this is necessary. Marshall would have been happy here. The final fishery of note belongs to Lord Palumbo. It is of 2 miles (3.2 km), down to Bagnor and is the only fishery on the river to have a full-time keeper. Such keepering as is done above is on an informal basis, by the members or the fishery owner. Lord Palumbo, who is Chairman of the Arts Council, keeps the fishing for his friends and guests.

At Bagnor there is a fish farm, and from here down the Lambourn is in a sorry state, which, as reported in *The Times*, has greatly distressed the distinguished actor, Sir Michael Hordern, who has known and loved the river for 40 years. At Bagnor itself, one carrier is dry. Below at Donnington, where the Piscatorials used to lease the water from the Gladstone family (descendants of the great Victorian Prime Minister) the lake is now stagnant and the river, which flows well enough, is not fished because the whole Donnington estate has been bought by a Japanese company, who plan to make a golf course and country hotel. The Piscatorial Society had this water for more than 70 years. They managed it to a high standard, but they gave it up in the late seventies because of the nuisance of escapee rainbows from the fish farm, a deterioration in water quality, the encroachment of Newbury out to Donnington, and the fact that superior water became available on the Wylye. A final nail in the coffin will be the new A34 dual carriageway outer ring road, which will pass between Bagnor and Donnington.

It is far from true to say that the Lambourn is ruined. Certainly below Bagnor it is, but that is only a very small part of the river. Above Great Shefford it is almost dry, but that has always been so after a dry winter. Between Great Shefford and Bagnor there is several miles of splendid fishing for wild trout. Walking along some of the major chalk streams, while researching for this book, I felt no desire to fish. It was too artificial in every way. But on the little Lambourn my hand itched to hold a rod and stalk those wily fish which sidled away under the weed as I appeared.

THE PANG

The full course of the little Pang is 14 miles (22.5 km). It flows in a great loop – south from Compton, east below Frilsham, north from the M4 to the Thames at Pangbourne. At the time of writing (summer 1991) the top 7 miles (11.2 km) are dry: but there is every hope that by the time these words are read, it will be flowing again over its full course.

THE PANG

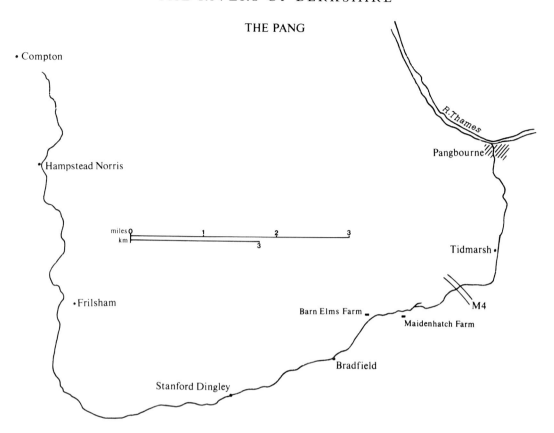

The Pang is an interesting river, which like so many has suffered grievously from the effects of abstraction, and has found dedicated supporters to fight for it. In one welcome respect it is unique. Its supporters claim that they have won the battle. The Pang's troubles began in the early seventies, when the then Thames Water Authority were authorised to abstract 13½ million litres a day from a borehole at Compton, to supply Didcot, which is northwards, and thus the water was lost to the Pang. The result was that the top seven miles (11.2 km) down to Stanford Dingley dried up completely. Led by Mr Peter Trentham, the Pang Valley Conservation Trust fought a long battle, and Thames Water plc have now agreed to reduce the abstraction to 5 million litres a day from the end of 1991, which Mr Trentham thinks is acceptable, given normal rainfall. They have been fortunate in that Thames Water have found an alternative source further up the Thames, so that the question of compensation has not arisen.

'We have tried not to antagonise people,' said Mr Trentham, 'and we have had the best possible co-operation from the NRA and the water company.' There is a lesson here – undue belligerence can be self-defeating.

The first real sight of the Pang at present is at the attractive village of Stanford Dingley, where it flows through some typically English well-tended private gardens. Within half a mile (.8 km) is the first fishery, at Kimberhead Farm, where there is the well-known Blue Pool. Here, water bubbles up from springs in the chalk and has never failed even in the worst drought, and has sustained the Pang below. A syndicate has a stretch, which they stock, of about a mile (1.6 km). It is a tiny stream here, not more than 6 ft (.8 m) wide, heavily wooded and challenging fishing.

Below this is a mile belonging to Bradfield College, the public school well known for staging Greek plays. The Pang is bigger here, some 20 ft (6.0 m) wide, but canal like and sluggish, which has resulted in a build-up of silt and ribbon weed. It is somewhat neglected, but a master keen on fishing has recently arrived and if he provides leadership there are always boys willing to help to put the river in order. It needs to be narrowed, to increase the flow, and I would certainly suggest lowering the hatches. Better a low river in good shape than a high one silted up.

Next comes the Barn Elms water, rather similar, where a syndicate has a mile, and there is also a 6½-acre (2.6 ha) lake offering stillwater fishing for rainbows. The setting is most attractive, and it is popular. Below this is another syndicate at Maidenhatch Farm, who also have a mile (1.6 km) down to just above the M4 crossing.

Up to the M4, the Pang is a pretty river, flowing through rural Berkshire, peaceful and unspoilt. But after Maidenhatch the river flows under the M4 and the A340 Pangbourne to Theale road. It then runs parallel to, and within 200 yards (182.8 m) of, the A340 – which must be one of the busiest roads in England. There are two fisheries here, one operated by the Englefield Estate and the other a syndicate on water belonging to Mr Michael Metcalfe.

After Maidenhatch, just before the place where the Pang runs under the M4, the Englefield Estate have about ¾ mile (1.2 km) with good mayfly and the usual chalk stream flies. It is lightly fished, with two rods fishing two days a week, and two fishing one day a week plus friends of the Estate. It is stocked with 150 browns up to 1½ lb (.68 kg). A rainbow of 5 in. (12.5 cm) was caught in 1991. Although Maidenhatch stock with rainbows, this small fish was almost certainly bred in the river. Rainbows have been known to breed naturally in chalk streams, but the population never establishes itself – fortunately, for if they did, the future for the brown would be bleak.

The last fishery is that of Mr Michael Metcalfe, which has about ¾ mile (1.2 km). They stock with one third rainbows and two thirds browns, up to 1½ lb (.68 kg), and is fished by a dozen season rods. In the summer of 1991, the water level is low, with silt and lack of weed. Normally there is good dry fly fishing on this stretch, but they suffer from poaching, especially during the school holidays.

I look forward to returning to the Pang in a year's time, to see it once again flowing through the villages of Hampstead Norreys and Frilsham, where Mr Ted Pope, who keepers several stretches, remembers seeing wild four-pounders (1.8 kg). What joy that will bring to Peter Trentham and all those who have fought for their river.

There is still open country between Pangbourne and its large neighbour Reading, and it remains a pleasant little Berkshire town. Kenneth Graham, author of the *Wind in the Willows*, lived in Pangbourne. People will point out Ratty's hole, near the Blue Pool. The inhabitants of Tidmarsh say that Graham used to walk up there, sit on the river bank, and dream about the adventures of Mole, Ratty, and Badger – to which he added the character who made the book immortal – Toad of Toad Hall.

THE LODDON

The Loddon rises in Basingstoke and enters the Thames at Shiplake, a full course of about 25 miles (40.2 km). Only the top mile (1.6 km) from the source is pure chalk: after that it has a bed of clay and is a coarse fishing river. But there is an intermediate area between the pure chalk and the clay, where fly fishing is possible and there are two major fisheries. I have included the Loddon as a Berkshire river because most of its course is in that county, but it so happens that the fly fishing part is in Hampshire.

The first fishery is that of the Gresham Angling Club, of long and honourable pedigree. It was founded in 1881, in the City of London, and numbered R. B. Marston among its founder members. Marston was also a founder member of the Flyfishers Club and Editor of the *Fishing Gazette*, the leading angling magazine of the Victorian era. They fished on the Coln, near Slough and on the Thames, which used to produce enormous trout from pools below the weirs. In 1955, when this had

THE RIVER LODDON
(chalk stream section only)

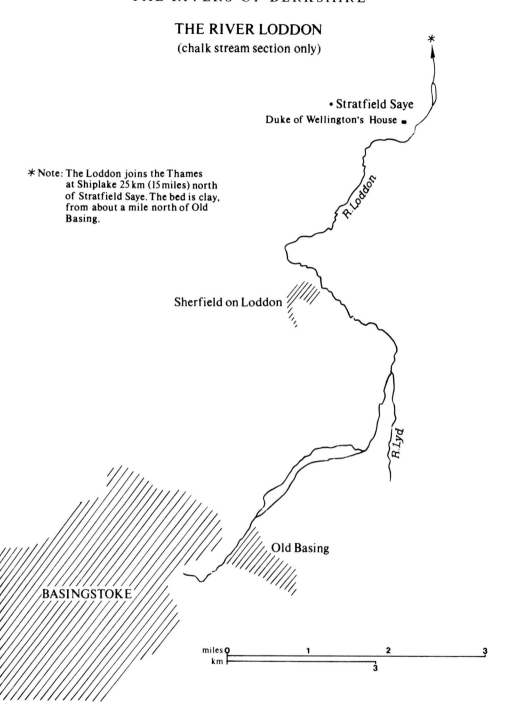

∗ Note: The Loddon joins the Thames
at Shiplake 25 km (15 miles) north
of Stratfield Saye. The bed is clay,
from about a mile north of Old
Basing.

• Stratfield Saye
Duke of Wellington's House ■

R. Loddon

Sherfield on Loddon

R. Lyd

Old Basing

BASINGSTOKE

miles 0   1   2   3
km   3

deteriorated, they took their present water on the Loddon and its little tributary the Lyd (pronounced 'lied').

The 40 members have 4½ miles (7.2 km) of fishing, including a mile of the Lyd, between Old Basing and Sherfield on Loddon. Considering the nearness of the monstrous concrete sprawl of Basingstoke, I was astonished at the old world tranquility of Basing and the fine condition of the Loddon.

The top mile of the Gresham water is a typical clear chalk stream – only some ten feet (3 m), wide, but with a good flow over gravel and plentiful ranunculus and water celery. There are even wild trout here, supplemented by stocked browns up to 1½ lb (.68 kg). Kingfishers flash down the stream with rosebay willow-herb along the banks. Basingstoke could be a hundred miles away.

After this first mile of chalk, clay begins to appear. The river is bigger, less clear, and more sluggish, with signs of ribbon weed.

But it is still good fishing, though there is no natural spawning and the policy is to stock with rainbows. It is still rural and quiet, and the river winds about pleasantly. The Lyd is similar – pure chalk at the top, clay and sluggish lower down.

The members of the Gresham Club are all season members. They can fish either two days a week, or three part days, defined as up to four hours. It is a fine club, well run and the river is not over fished. The fact that the Loddon has not been ruined by abstraction from Basingstoke – that it flourishes – seems to me almost miraculous.

Downstream of Sherfield is the Duke of Wellington's Stratfield Saye estate, including 4½ miles (7.3 km) of flyfishing on the Loddon. The house, which was given to the first Duke by the nation after Waterloo, is open to the public.

The river here is as big as the upper Itchen, and quite attractive with good ranunculus and gravel bottom. Weirs help to oxygenate the water. One bank has been left wild and the other has been mown like a lawn so that casting is easy. In my opinion, it is too easy. It is manicured. The river is divided into five beats. One angler fishes each beat every day – thus, there are 35 rods. If there is a vacancy, day tickets are issued. The bag limit is six fish per angler per day. The river is stocked with 75 per cent browns and 25 per cent rainbows from 1¼ lb to 6 lb (.56 to 2.72 kg). Stocking takes place every three weeks during the season: in total, they stock about 4,000 fish.

It is a put-and-take fishery, run as a business, and the river is put under severe pressure. No doubt it contributes a handsome profit to the coffers of the Stratfield Saye estate, and no doubt many anglers enjoy it. But it saddens me to see any river treated in this way.

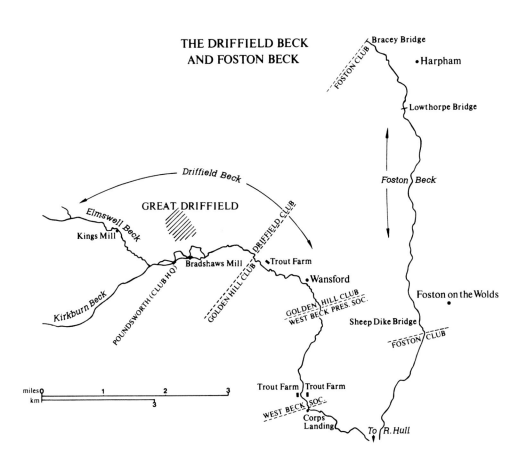

THE DRIFFIELD BECK
AND FOSTON BECK

Bracey Bridge

•Harpham

FOSTON CLUB

Lowthorpe Bridge

Driffield Beck

Foston Beck

Elmswell Beck

GREAT DRIFFIELD

Kings Mill

DRIFFIELD CLUB

•Trout Farm

Bradshaws Mill

•Wansford

POUNDSWORTH (CLUB HQ)

Kirkburn Beck

GOLDEN HILL CLUB

GOLDEN HILL CLUB
WEST BECK PRES. SOC.

Foston on the Wolds
•

Sheep Dike Bridge

FOSTON CLUB

miles 0   1   2   3

km   3

Trout Farm Trout Farm

WEST BECK SOC.

Corps
Landing

To R. Hull

6

THE RIVERS OF
YORKSHIRE

Driffield Beck

Foston Beck

Those who fish the southern chalk streams may know little about the chalk streams in Yorkshire. However, they may well have heard of the old-established and rather exclusive club – the Driffield Anglers Club – and a fly named the Driffield Dun. But of the streams themselves, the fishing, the countryside, the history, and the current problems, practically nothing is known outside the East Riding of Yorkshire.

There are good reasons for this. Over the last forty years, they have been wary of publicity, fearing the damage it might do to a small and precious resource. But they are coming to see that publicity may be necessary, to mobilise public opinion to prevent further damage to these beautiful streams. For there has been great damage in recent years, and it must be stopped.

There are only two streams – the Driffield Beck (providing about 16 miles/25.7 km of chalk stream fishing) and the Foston Beck, which has about six miles (9.8 km) of fishing. They are both near the town of Great Driffield (pop. 9,000), about 25 miles (40.2 km) to the north of Kingston upon Hull. Both flow into the river Hull.

As the map (see page 152) shows, the Driffield rises west of Great Driffield in two feeder streams, the Elmswell and the Kirkburn, which join at Poundsworth Mill, flowing eastwards to the village of Wansford, then turning south until it joins the Hull. The Foston Beck rises at Kilham, about 5 miles (8.0 km) east of Great Driffield, and flows south until it, too, joins the Hull. Only the top six miles (9.6 km) is chalk.

THE DRIFFIELD BECK

C. F. Walker, in *An Anglers Odyssey* (1958), described the Driffield as 'a river of surprises, constantly changing character'. From the source to Bradshaws Mill, he wrote, it descends through a little valley, with broad swift shallows and deeper stretches like the upper Itchen.

As I saw it, in mid May, with the willows and alders in their fresh green leaves, with the golden buttercups, the yellow cowslips, and the silver lady smock, it was indeed as J. W. Hills said in *My Sporting Life* (1936) 'a little bit of Hampshire put down in Yorkshire'. Below Bradshaws Mill, the scene changes to flat grazing land, sparse of trees and bushes and any kind of cover. It is drained marsh, for the soil is black peat, like the Fens. With the herds of Friesians, it could almost be Holland. Maurice Headlam (*Rod Horn and Gun*, 1942) said that the scene had great charm with snipe and duck winging overhead, the clear stream winding through the meadows, and no hint of human life until you lift your eyes and see a sail slowly crawling above apparently dry land behind the clump of trees by the Hull canal.

Fifty years later, some of the charm is gone. Ugly pylons march across the meadows, a favourite perch for cormorants, and three large fish farms with their industrial buildings, disfigure the scene. Of this, more later. And the Hull canal has fallen into disuse. But one asset remains – the remarkable clarity of the water. On the bends, it is often 6 ft (1.82 km) deep, but the white chalk bed reflects every inch of the water. Trout can be seen many yards ahead and this makes them extremely shy and provides a stern test of the anglers skill. I have not seen water of such clarity in 1991 in any of the southern rivers.

Apart from about a half a mile (.8 km) of the Elmswell Beck, which is privately owned, all the water down to Whin Hill, about ten miles (16 km), is fished by the Driffield Anglers Club. Below that, the Golden Hill Club has some 2½ miles (4.0 km), followed by the West Beck Preservation Society with about the same down to Corpslanding, where the chalk ends. We will consider the three clubs, starting at the bottom with the West Beck.

This is an old established club, of at least fifty years, with 25 members. They rely on stocked fish, two thirds browns and one third rainbows, of about 1¼ lb (.56 kg). It is flat and open country, windswept at times, and they are beset by problems. At the bottom of the fishery are two medium-sized fish farms on opposite banks, which are in fierce competition with each other for the available water.

During the drought years of 1989 and 1990, they have been leap frogging up each bank with their water intakes, until one

Bringing in a trout on the Driffield and West Beck.

was two thirds up the West Beck Club's water. After protests, they were forced by the NRA to retreat, and now the top intake is about half-way up. Below this the river was so denuded it was unfishable in 1990.

As if this was not enough, there is a plague of cormorants. And in 1982 there was a major pollution by pig slurry. Dr Robert Blair, the Chairman, believes it harmed the fly life, which has not fully recovered. At the beginning of the 1991 season the river is flowing well and the water, if somewhat bare of weed, still has its brilliant clarity. If there is a wet summer, fishing will be possible. If there is a drought, it will not.

Next upstream is the Golden Hill Club with about 2½ miles (4.0 km) of similar water with similar problems. The river meanders pleasantly through the flat plain and the Club, in the person of its long-standing and devoted secretary, Mr Denis Whitham, are planting willows along the banks to provide cover. They have also prevailed upon the farmer to fence off his cattle, leaving a wide path along the banks, which are otherwise trampled down. Mr Witham pointed out eight cormorants, sitting on a pylon. 'A fortnight ago, I put 50 fish into a pool. Now, there is not one left – the cormorants have had the lot. There are not enough fish left in the North Sea, so they come here.'

But the Wansford Fish Farm, producing 600 tonnes a year and one of the biggest in England, is an even worse problem, for its intake is at the top of the Golden Hill water. The farm has been prosecuted and fined three times, either for exceeding their discharge consent or for taking more water than they are permitted. The ACA and Mr Whitham together have fought a long, hard, fight. The last time, the farm was fined £7,000 plus costs, and there are now signs that they are, at last, putting their house in order. It was madness ever to have allowed such a large fish farm on a river like the Driffield Beck, which is roughly the

The West Beck below Wansford. The beck here is flat and open but the water is crystal clear – a true chalk stream.

size of the Wylye, and has nothing like the flow of the Test below Stockbridge or the Avon below Salisbury.

The Golden Hill Club have twenty members, they care for their water well, and it is not over-fished. There are welcome signs of ranunculus appearing, and in May 1991 it was fishing well. Once again, all depends on the rainfall in the next few months.

Finally, we come to the Driffield Anglers Club, with their ten miles of fishing, founded in 1833, and the second oldest fishing club in England. The Houghton Club is eleven years older. It is the most carefully preserved of the three clubs, with two full-time keepers, a fine club house, and is the only one where wild trout remain.

It was the top part of the water, the two feeder streams (Elmswell and Kirkburn) and the main river down to Bradshaws, which J. W. Hills had in mind when he compared the Driffield with the upper Itchen. He added 'on a lower emotional plane', a very personal comment. I suspect it was a reference to the long associations that the Itchen had for him. He was ecstatic about the fly life. 'Fly was wonderfully plentiful in 1920. It was there in masses, sometimes twenty or thirty in a square foot . . . even when trout were feeding hard, they could not eat more than one in ten . . . yet even that was nothing compared to what I had seen on September 12, 1919. Never on any river have I seen such a sight, nor do I believe has anyone else. For nearly two hours the water was discoloured with fly. They were there in hundreds of thousands. And I never got a fish!'

Apart from Hills, others commented on the marvellous fly hatches – Halford in 1891, Anthony Buxton between the wars, Arthur Oglesby and Donald Overfield in the sixties. In 1991, it is still dry fly water, but the teeming hatches are no more. It may be the lack of ranunculus. It may be agricultural sprays. It may be the effect of the pig slurry pollution of 1982. No one can be sure.

But it is good to know that there are still wild trout to be found. The club stock with about 400 takeable browns, from their own hatchery, but the annual catch is about 1,000.

There is a famous fly, the Driffield Dun. Courtney Williams simply calls it 'an old north country fly'. Hills used it in 1919, though he had more success with a Halford blue-winged olive. It looks rather like a Greenwells Glory. I had expected it to be the most popular fly, and was a little disappointed to find that it is not. It is still used, but in conjunction with the usual southern flies – Greenwells, Black Gnat, Lunns Particular, etc. I accepted gratefully the offer to cast a fly on these hallowed waters, and managed to catch a trout of about 1 lb (.45 kg) on my favourite Adams. It was a beautiful yellow, silvery fish, full of fight, the light colouring, I imagine, to tone in with the white chalk gravel of the bottom.

There is conflicting advice about striking. Hills says that it is difficult to be too slow. C. F. Walker says that you need to strike quicker than on southern streams, and that is the consensus of informed opinion today.

Below Bradshaws, the water changes character and becomes flat and open, like that of Golden Hill and West Beck. In 1990,

Dawson's Dam stretch of the Driffield.

only the water below Bradshaws was fishable after June. The lovely stretches above dried up to a trickle. The trouble here is not fish farms, but extraction by borehole, much of it by farmers for spray irrigation, under licenses granted many years ago, when it was thought there was a limitless supply. They are licenses 'of right', which means that if revoked, compensation will be payable. For this to happen, there will have to be a ground swell of public opinion to force the Government to act.

By the kindness of Mr Stephen Madden, the Chairman, I was able to see a copy of the Club history, compiled by Donald Overfield. It is leather bound, but in typescript, and the copy I saw belonged to Sir Thomas Ferens, the President, who is in his eighties and unfortunately in poor health. There is an early entry

Stephen Madden, Chairman of the Driffield Anglers Club, on the Driffield Beck. J. W. Hills described this as 'a little bit of Hampshire put down in Yorkshire'.

from Hofland's *British Anglers Manual* (1839). After stating that a trout of 17 lb (7.7 kg) had been caught in 1832, Hofland says 'I am informed that a club has been established for the preservation of this superior breed of fish.' The club was indeed established in 1833, with 40 members, mostly local landowners but including two sporting parsons.

In *An Anglers Autobiography* (1903), F. M. Halford wrote, in his prosaic way: 'In 1891, I had good sport casting over rising fish using ordinary Hampshire patterns. In eight days, I killed 37 fish weighing 39 lb 11 oz.' The Driffield Dun is first mentioned in 1922, in an article in the *Flyfishers Journal*. There are said to be archives and documents in a trunk in Sir Thomas' house which have not yet been examined. Until they are, we know little of the early years. The present history really begins with the arrival of Sir Thomas as a young member during the last war, when the river was being poached, using hand grenades, by crews from a nearby Bomber Command base. In his memoir, he writes: 'Looking back, we could not grudge them their delicacy, when in a few hours they would be off on a flight from which many would never return.' I was sorry not to be able to meet a man of such generous spirit.

In 1950, there was an extraordinary AGM. The river had suffered so badly, during the war, from poaching and neglect, that the general opinion was that it had either to be put right, or the club wound up. Sir Thomas brought Alf Lunn (father of Mick, son of William) up from the Houghton Club to report and advise. His report was comprehensive, the members accepted it and agreed to put up the finance. Sir Thomas engaged six men, and supervised the work himself. Within a year, the river was back to its former glory.

In 1954, Mr Addington of Scarborough, a long-time member, then aged 91, had a heart attack on the river. On his deathbed in hospital, he called for Sir Thomas and said that he wanted to thank him for all he had done for the stream in repairing the neglect of the war, and that the recent seasons had been the best ever. In 1961, Sir Thomas, who owned the local estate, found that he had Poundsworth Mill cottage vacant, and gave it to the club as a keeper's cottage and club room. It is a splendid room, with lawns sloping down to the mill pool, in every way ideal for the purpose. Thus, from 1961 onwards, the club had no need to go to a hotel for their annual dinner: they had their own home.

The question of Lady Members is one which is topical today, and can generate strong feelings. The story of how the Driffield Club grappled with it is told by Mr D. H. Crockett in the history. The first Lady Member was as early as 1918 – Mrs Claude Reynard, wife of one President and daughter-in-law of another. In 1933, Mrs Vernon Holt, wife of a President, became the second.

The matter did not arise again until 1965, when Mrs Allan Crockett fished as a guest. Seeing her skill, Sir Thomas said there were precedents and she might become a member. But by this time, the club had its Poundsworth Mill HQ, and the social side was more important. When the subject came up for discussion, some members demurred. The ladies might take over the club room for afternoon bridge. Or, horror of horrors, they might sunbathe on the banks in bikinis and frighten the fish. Sir Thomas effected a compromise. Mrs Crockett would become a Lady Associate Member, without voting rights, and so would not attend the AGM or the Annual Dinner, which would remain all male. Mrs Crockett commented: 'I am only the third fish wife in 136 years.'

Just when it seemed that all the problems had been overcome, a major and unforeseen dilemma arose. A challenge cup was presented every year at the Annual Dinner to the member who had caught the biggest fish. In 1969, Mrs Crockett led the field. Her husband fished long and hard to try to beat her, but failed by 3 oz (85 g). Given that no one – male or female – wanted the Annual Dinner to be mixed, but that by tradition the cup had to be presented at the dinner, the problem seemed intractable. But not to the supreme diplomat, Sir Thomas Ferens, who arranged for a sherry party to take place between the AGM and the Annual Dinner, at which the cup would be presented.

Since then, Lady Associate Members have become uncontroversial. There are three at present. They still win the cup!

FOSTON BECK

Like the Driffield, but smaller, the Foston Beck has two distinct characteristics. Above Lowthorpe it is idyllic, meandering through woods running clear and strong, with as good a growth of ranunculus as I have seen anywhere. Below Lowthorpe it is less attractive, running slow and deep between high banks, with too much silt and mud. It looks as if it was once part of an old irrigation system. The Foston Club has, among its 23 members, some who are young and active, and they have done excellent work putting in weirs to clear away the silt and mud, and oxygenate the water. I was told that it still provides good fishing, though only for stocked fish.

J. W. Hills had some good days on the Foston in 1920. The Lowthorpe water, he said, was as good a water for catching fish

Weirs above Lowthorpe on the Foston Beck, where fly hatches are still good.

as anywhere in England. The marvellous thing about it, he added, was that any fish that was visible could be induced to rise. And the fly life was prolific, though not so exceptional as on the Driffield.

Nowadays, the fly life is not so exceptional on either stream, and in 1990, due to lack of water, the Foston was unfishable. In May 1991, it was running well, and the fishermen on it were happy.

CONCLUSION

We hear much of the decline of the southern chalk streams but the fact is that the Yorkshire streams have suffered worse. In 1990, about 10 per cent of the southern streams were unfishable. In Yorkshire, it was at least 40 per cent. If wet winters and summers ever return, there will be an improvement. But I cannot see these rivers ever regaining their quality while the three fish farms remain on the Driffield and abstraction continues at the present rate.

In *A Fisherman's Diary* (1969), Oliver Kite wrote: 'The fishing throughout was excellent, the company delightful, and I came away spiritually refreshed and physically in excellent form. Now that is just what fishing should do to a man.' Those were my impressions also, in May 1991. There was a cruel irony about Kite's remark about his physical condition, for his book was published posthumously – an example I hope not to follow.

There is another memory, with which I should like to end this account. The writers of the past, like Grey or Skues, used to speak of the pellucid waters of the Test or the Itchen. Seeing the Yorkshire streams, which like the southern streams have lost so much in volume, made me appreciate what that word – pellucid – really means. The brilliant clarity of the water is what I shall remember. It makes the southern streams look dirty.

FLY DRESSINGS

DRY FLIES

Greenwell's Glory
BODY: Waxed yellow tying silk, ribbed fine gold wire
WINGS: Darkest starling or hen blackbird wing feather
HACKLE: Light furnace cock's

Orange Quill (H. H. Brayshaw)
TAIL: Orange hackle fibres
BODY: Quill dyed orange
WINGS: Rusty dun hackle points
HACKLE: Orange

Ginger Quill
TAIL: Ginger cock hackle fibres
BODY: Undyed peacock quill from the eye
HACKLE: Ginger cock

Lunn's Particular (W. Lunn)
TAIL: Four fibres of natural red from large hackle
BODY: Undyed hackle stalks from natural Rhode Island Red cock hackle
WINGS: Two medium blue dun cock hackle points put on flat
HACKLE: Natural red
TYING SILK: Dark red

Houghton Ruby (W. Lunn)
TAIL: Three fibres from white cock hackle
BODY: Rhode Island hackle stalk dyed red
WINGS: Two light blue dun hen tips from the breast or back set on flat
HACKLE: Bright Rhode Island red hackle
TYING SILK: Dark red

Caperer (W. Lunn)
BODY: Four or five strands from Cinnamon turkey tail feather, two strands from swan feather, dyed yellow to make a ring of yellow in the centre of the body
WINGS: Coot, bleached and dyed chocolate brown
HACKLE: One medium Rhode Island cock hackle, one black cock hackle put in front of wings
TYING SILK: Crimson

Black Gnat (Roger Woolley)
BODY: Black quill or black silk
HACKLE: Black cock

Adams (Ray Bergman, USA)

TAIL: Fibres of grizzle hackles
BODY: Blue grey wool or fur
WINGS: Two grizzle hackles tied spent
HACKLE: Red grizzle cock

Driffield Dun

TAIL: Pale ginger cock fibres
BODY: Pale blue fur, ribbed yellow tying silk
WINGS: Tied forward, pale starling
HACKLE: Pale ginger cock

Iron Blue (Harry Powell)

TAIL: Iron blue hackle fibres
BODY: Mole fur dubbing
HACKLE: Iron blue

Terry's Terror (Dr Cecil Terry)

BODY: One strand of bronze peacock herl twisted with yellow tying silk
RIB: very fine flat copper tinsel
TAIL: a stubby one, consisting of equal parts of orange and yellow bucktail hair
HACKLE: medium red cock

Beacon Beige (Peter Deane)

BODY: Stripped peacock quill from the eye feather with clearly defined markings so that it produces a nice ribbing effect. One has seen the quill over-tied on a floss base but this is not in the original dressing
WHISKS: Four or five fibres from a stiff grizzle cock
HACKLES: Grizzle, with a dark red cock wound through it. The original dressing specified a very springy Indian red game hackle, dark, and rather long in the fibre

Cinnamon Sedge (Roger Woolley)

BODY: A strand from a cinnamon turkey tail feather, ribbed gold wire
BODY HACKLE: Ginger cock's
SHOULDER HACKLE: Ginger cock's tied in front of wings
WINGS: Landrail wing feather

Hawthorn (Roger Woolley)

BODY: Two black strands from a turkey tail feather, tied in so that the bright black quill of them shows up most. The ends of the two strands are tied back after forming the body to represent the two long trailing legs of the fly
HACKLE: Black cock
WINGS: Palest part of jay wing feather

Grey Wulff (Lee Wulff)

SILK: Brown
TAIL: Bucktail fibres or squirrel-tail fibres
BODY: Grey rabbit fur
WINGS: Bucktail tied pointing forward and up, and split in a 'V'
HACKLE: Blue dun cock

Deerstalker (Neil Patterson)

SILK: Brown
TAIL: Pheasant-tail fibres, a full inch (2.5 cm) long
BODY: A bunch of deerhair whipped to the shank, the points just projecting beyond the bend of the hook, ribbed with tying silk and fine silver wire
HACKLE: Black cock wound and trimmed to form a thorax. A large red cock hackle wound on and tied 'spent' into two bunches

Blue-winged Olive Dun (Lapsley)

SILK: Yellow

TAIL: Pale blue-dun cock hackle fibres

BODY: Tying silk lightly dubbed with 50/50 mix of olive and brown seal's fur

HACKLE: Blue-dun cock and red-brown cock wound together

Pheasant Tail Red Spinner (Kite)

SILK: Red

TAIL: White

BODY AND THORAX: Pheasant-tail herls

HACKLE: Dark red

Hooks

Up-eyed for dry flies; **down-eyed** for nymphs

SIZES 12–14 on large rivers; 16–18 (or even smaller) on small streams; 8–10 for Mayflies

---

NYMPHS

Hatching Nymphs or Emergers

Gold-ribbed Hare's Ear (GRHE)

ABDOMEN: Hare or rabbit fur ribbed with fine gold wire

TAIL WHISKS: None, or a few short dun hackle-fibres

THORAX: A slightly thicker dubbing of hare or rabbit fur

HACKLE: One turn, two at the most, of a short dun hackle

Midge Pupa

SILK: Black

TAIL: White cock's hackle fibres cut to ⅛ inch (3 mm)

ABDOMEN: Black or dark olive floss silk ribbed with fine silver wire

THORAD: Peacock herl

BREATHING FILAMENTS: White DRF wool, clipped short

Sunk Nymphs

Pheasant Tail (Sawyer)

Wire body: Cover the hook evenly from head to bend with fine copper wire, then build up a wire thorax, returning the wire to the hook-bend

Body covering: Using the wire as you would tying silk, tie in four red-coloured fibres at the bend, the fibres projecting no more than 1/8 of an inch (3 mm) beyond the bend. These represent the tails of the nymph. Spin the fibres round the wire and cover the body to the eye of the hook with the mixed fibres and wire. At the hook eye, separate the fibres and wire. Place the wire behind the thorax. Bend the fibres back from the hook eye over the thorax and trap them behind with the wire

Finish with a half-hitch on the wire, or, alternatively, four turns. Break off the wire, and varnish. Alternatively return the wire and fibres from behind the thorax to the eye of the hook and trim off by the eye

Grey Goose (Sawyer)

Construction, as for Pheasant Tail except:

a wire golden, not copper

b use herls from wing feathers or ordinary grey goose.

Note: Both Pheasant Tail and Grey Goose, if tied with silk instead of wire, can be used as Hatching Nymphs

FLY PATTERNS

EARLY SEASON

Natural			Artificial	
	Dun	*Spinner*	*Hatching Nymph*	*Sunk Nymph*
Hawthorn		Hawthorn		
Large Dark Olive	Greenwells Glory or Beacon Beige	PT★ Red Spinner	GRHE★	PT Nymph
Mayfly	Grey Wulff	Deerstalker		
Iron Blue	Iron Blue	Houghton Ruby	GRHE★ or PT Nymph (silk tied)	PT Nymph
Medium Olive	Greenwells or Adams	Lunn's Particular	GRHE or PT Nymph (silk tied)	PT Nymph
Black Gnat		Black Gnat		
Midge Pupa			Midge Pupa	

FLY DRESSINGS

MID SEASON

Pale Watery	Ginger Quill	Lunn's Particular	Grey Goose (silk tied)	Grey Goose
Blue-Winged Olive	BWO★ Dun	Orange Quill	GRHE	PT Nymph
Sedges		Cinnamon Sedge		
plus Midge Pupa and Black Gnat				

LATE SEASON

As for mid-season, plus Large Dark Olive and Iron Blue,
which re-appear, and Caperer for daytime sedges in September.

NOTES

The above list is a general guide. Certain patterns do well on certain rivers and are given with the river.

Size of fly is important. A good guide is the nearer the source of the river, the smaller the fly.

With one exception, all the above are traditional chalk stream flies. The exception is the Adams, an American fly which is increasing in popularity. It is easily visible, even when one's eyes are tired, it sits up well, and the fish seem to find it attractive.

★ Abbreviations: PT = Pheasant Tail
                        GRHE = Gold Ribbed Hare's Ear
                        BWO = Blue-Winged Olive

BIBLIOGRAPHY

A Personal Selection

'How-to-fish' Books

Dry Fly Fishing, F. M. Halford (1889, reprinted with Foreword by Dermot Wilson, 1989, Witherby)

Minor Tactics of the Chalk Stream, G. E. M. Skues (A. & C. Black, 1910)

The Way of a Trout with a Fly, G. E. M. Skues (A. & C. Black, 1921)

Nymphs and the Trout, Frank Sawyer (A. & C. Black, 1970)

Fishing the Dry Fly, Dermot Wilson (3rd Edition, revised 1987, Unwin Hyman)

River Trout Fishing, Peter Lapsley (Unwin Hyman, 1988)

'Fireside' Books

Where the Bright Waters Meet, Harry Plunket Greene (Philip Allan, 1924)

A Summer on The Test, John Waller Hills (Hodder & Stoughton, 1924)

Reflections on a River, Howard Marshall (Witherby, 1967)

Fly Fishing, Sir Edward Grey (Dent, 1907)

A Particular Lunn, Mick Lunn with Clive Graham-Ranger (Unwin Hyman, 1990)

Keeper of the Stream, Frank Sawyer (A. & C. Black, 1952; Unwin Hyman, 1985)

Nature Diary, Janet Marsh (Michael Joseph, 1979)

Biography

G. E. M. Skues, The Way of a Man with a Trout, Donald Overfield (Benn, 1977)

Frank Sawyer, Man of the Riverside, Frank Sawyer and Sidney Vines (Unwin Hyman, 1984; paperback, 1987)

Fly-dressing and Entomology

Waterside Guide, John Goddard (Unwin Hyman, 1988)

Fly Dresser's Guide, John Veniard (A. & C. Black, 1952)

Fly Tying Techniques, Jacqueline Wakeford (Benn, 1980)

A Dictionary of Trout Flies, A Courtney Williams (paperback, 6th Edn., A. & C. Black, 1986)

Historical

A History of Fly Fishing for Trout, John Waller Hills (Philip Allan, 1921)

The Fishing in Print, Arnold Gingrich (Winchester Press, 1974)

Note: Out-of-print books can be obtained from John & Judith Head, The Barn Book Supply, 88 Crane Street, Salisbury, Wiltshire SP1 2QD (Tel: 0722-327767).

USEFUL ADDRESSES

───── **FISHERIES OFFERING DAY TICKETS** ─────

TEST

Longparish Estate	Mr Alf Harper (Keeper) Home Farm Cottage Longparish, nr Andover, Hants SP11 6QQ	Tel: 026 472 419
Middleton Estate	Mr Jeff Smith (Keeper) Fishery Lodge Forton, Longparish, nr Andover, Hants SP11 6NU	Tel: 026 472 393
Wherwell Estate	Wherwell Estate Office Dublin Farm Wherwell, nr Andover, Hants	Tel: 0264 860243
Govett Estate (inc. Dever)	Mrs Govett Manor House Newton Stacey nr Stockbridge, Hants SO20 6BP	Tel: 0264 860630
Leckford Estate	Estate Office Leckford Stockbridge, Hants SO20 6JF	Tel: 0264 810634
Bossington Estate	Bossington Farms Ltd Houghton Stockbridge, Hants SO20 6LT	Tel: 0794 388265
Broadlands	Mr Bernard Aldrich (Keeper) Keepers Cottage Broadlands Estate Romsey, Hants	Tel: 0794 513052 *or* 0703 732354

USEFUL ADDRESSES

AVON	Avon Springs Fishing Lakes Ltd Recreation Rd Durrington Walls Salisbury, Wilts	Tel: 0980 53557
FROME	Dorchester Fishing Club J. J. Fisher (Hon Sec) Rew Hollow Godmanstone, Dorchester DT2 7AH	Tel: 0300 341306
	Mr R. Slocock Lawrences Farm Tolpuddle Dorchester DT2 7HF	Tel: 0305 848460
PIDDLE	Mr R. Slocock – details as above.	
ALLEN	Shaftesbury Estate Office Wimborne St Giles nr Wimborne, Dorset	Tel: 07254 214
	(Minimum of two days must be taken)	
KENNET	Denford Fisheries Tucketts, Lower Denford Hungerford, Berks RG17 0UN	Tel: 0488 684179 *or* 0488 58539
	Mr E. Hill Spinney House Barton Court Farm Kintbury, nr Newbury, Berks RG15 0SA	Tel: 0488 58226

handwritten annotations: John Aplin → 01305 - 357490 / 266500 Tu, th, Sat. B.H.   nhw dorchester fishing club   www go fly fishing

—— TACKLE SHOPS OFFERING FISHING ——

Rod Box	London Rd, Kings Worthy Winchester Hants SO23 7QN	Tel: 0962 883600

beats on the Test, Itchen, Nadder and Alre

Orvis Co Inc	The Mill, Nether Wallop Stockbridge Hants SO20 8ES	Tel: 0264 781212

beats on the Test and Itchen

FISHING ASSOCIATIONS

Test and Itchen Fishing Association Ltd.	Chairman: Mr John Potter Test Lodge, Houghton Stockbridge, Hants SO20 6LY	Tel: 0794 388352
	Secretary: Mr J. G. Glasspool West Haye Itcham Abbas Winchester SO21 1AX	Tel: 0962 78668
Wiltshire Fishery Association	Chairman: Col. C. L. Tarver MBE The Limes, Idmiston Rd Porton, Salisbury Wilts	Tel: 0980 610858
	Secretary: Col. A. V. Swindale 19 Fairfield Upavon, nr Pewsey Wilts	Tel: 0980 630535
Frome, Piddle & West Dorset Fishery Association	Chairman: Mr C. Rothwell c/o Weld Estates Secretary: Mr K. Lancaster Alpine Sunnyside West Lulworth Wareham Dorset BH20 5RU	Tel: 0929 41441
Kennet Valley Fishery Association	Chairman: G. J. Ward Esq CBE of Chilton Foliat Secretary: Mr P. G. Ludlow FSVA Lottage Waye Aldbourne Marlborough Wilts SN8 2EW	Tel: 0672 40375

SOME NOTABLE CLUBS

Dorchester Fishing Club
(0300 341306)

Frome

Sqn. Ldr. J. J. Fisher
Rew Hollow
Godmanstone
Dorchester DT2 7AH

Hungerford Town Fishery
(0488 682770)

Kennet, Dun

Lt. Col. D. Macey
100 High Street
Hungerford
Berks RG17 0NB

Gresham Angling Society
(0256 22515)

Loddon

Dr Alan Gibberd
Church Lane House
Old Basing, Hants
RG24 0DJ

Piscatorial Society
(038081 3357)

Avon, Wylye
Itchen

James Hunt Esq
Starlings, 76 High St
Market Lavington
Devizes, Wilts
SN10 4AG

Salisbury & Dist. AC
(0722 321164)

Avon, Wylye
Bourne

R. W. Hillier
29 New Zealand Ave
Salisbury, Wilts
SP2 7JX

Teffont Fishing Club
(0722 716463)

Nadder

Col. D. Lucas
Becketts, Chilmark
Salisbury, Wilts

Wilton Fly Fishing Club
(0952 52374)

Wylye

E. J. Hunt
Lee Mill Cottage
Leegomery, Telford
TF1 4QD

SERVICES CLUBS

Membership restricted to past or present members of the Services

Services Dry Fly Fishing Association (Upper Avon)
Secretary: Col. D. A. Miers, Tel: 0980 33371 Ext 2382
HQ Salisbury Plain Training Area, Bulford, Salisbury Wilts SP4 9PA

Portsmouth Services Fly Fishing Association (Meon and Itchen)
Secretary: Capt. F. Hefford RN, Tel: 0428 651440
20 Stoakley, Rise Haslemere, Surrey GU27 1AF

PRICE GUIDE

Prices given are for 1991 unless otherwise stated

Comparing one fishery with another simply on price can be misleading, because there are so many variables. For example:

(a) Length of river available. Better half a mile to yourself than a long stretch where there is always someone round the next bend.
(b) Fishing pressure. Is the river rested, or is it flogged seven days a week?
(c) Bag limit. Usually two brace. Catch and release?
(d) Guests. How many and how often?
(e) Rules as regards dry fly and nymph.
(f) Standard of upkeep, reflected in the general health of the river and the fly life.

Finally, the most individual factor of all – does the river and its setting appeal to you?

Where a comparison can be made, is between one river and another.

Examples of a Season Rod – one named day a week

Test £1500–£1000
Itchen £600–£500
Kennet £600–£500
Frome £350–£250
Wylye/Nadder £350–£250

Day Tickets

Day Tickets are often a disappointment. The conditions may be unsuitable, and one seldom does well the first day on a strange river. G.E.M. Skues said that he was just beginning to learn the Abbotts Barton water – and that was after 56 years! But it may be the only way to try out the chalk streams.

Examples of Day Tickets

Test	£90–£80
Itchen	Check with Rod Box or Orvis
Kennet	£30–£25
Avon	£20
Frome	£50–£15
Allen	£42
Piddle	£40–£30

Addresses and telephone numbers of fisheries who do Day Tickets are given in the section *Useful Addresses*. There are also advertisements in the angling press.

INDEX